The works of ANAIS NIN include two books of criticism, **D.H. Lawrence: An Unprofessional Study** and **Novel of the Future**; a prose poem, **House of Incest**; a collection of stories, **Under a Glass Bell**; seven novels, **Winter of Artifice, Spy in the House of Love, Ladders to Fire, Children of the Albatross, The Four Chambered Heart, Seduction of the Minotaur,** and **Collages;** four Volumes of the **Diary.**

ISBN: O-913660-04-3

Library of Congress Catalog Card Number: 73-81078

All material with the following exceptions copyright © by Valerie Harms, 1973. All rights reserved. No part of this book may be reproduced in any form without the written permission of the copyright holder.

Excerpts from The **Diary of Anais Nin** are reprinted by permission of Harcourt Brace Jovanovich, Inc.; copyright © 1966, 1967, 1969, by Anais Nin.

"The Poetic Reality of Anais Nin" by Anna Balakian was first presented at the Magic Circles' Weekend with Anais Nin in April, 1972 and subsequently published by Swallow Press in **The Anais Nin Reader.** It is hereby reprinted by permission of John Schaffner, Literary Agent. Copyright © 1973 by Anna Balakian.

SECOND PRINTING

Published by

MagiCircle PRESS
31 Chapel Lane
Riverside, Conn.
06878

Distributed by

J. Philip O'Hara, Inc.
20 East Huron
Chicago 60611
In Canada:
Van Nostrand Reinhold Ltd.
Scarborough, Ontario

CELEBRATION!
with
Anaïs Nin

photo by John Pearson

Editing with commentary and photography by

Valerie Harms

THE LOOK OF THE BOOK,
graphics, typography and layout
by
Adele Aldridge

This book is the record of an intimate weekend dialogue among thirty diverse strangers who came to meet one of this century's most original authors, Anais Nin, and some important persons from her life and work.

The instructive experiences of the Weekend, and the rich influence it had in many lives afterwards are herein presented for the public in the same spirit of celebration.

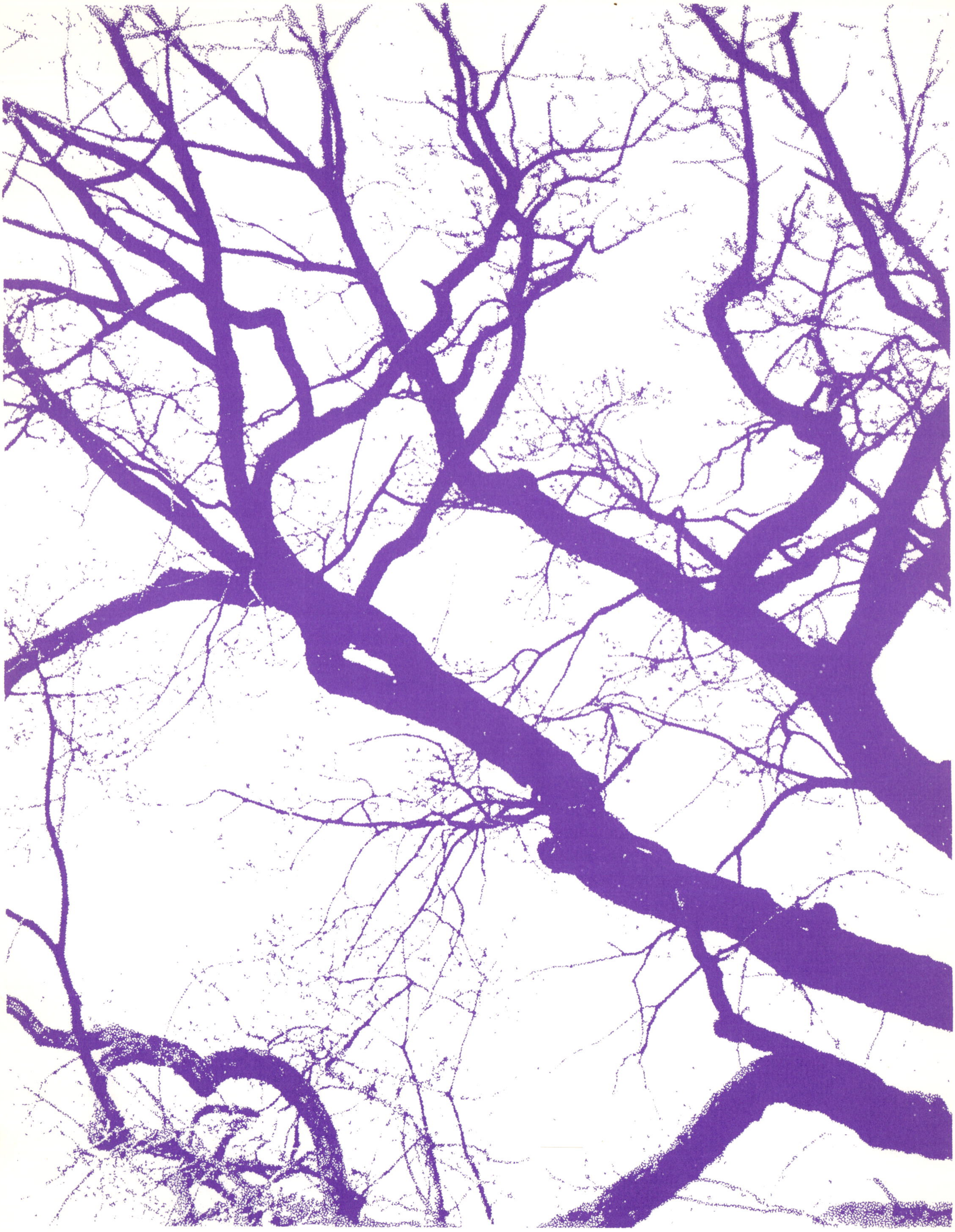

Contents

Preface by Evelyn J. Hinz - 1

Part I:
Circles and Dreams

1. The Cosmos of Anais Nin - 4
2. Magic Circles - 12

Part II:
The Living Dream Weekend

3. The Celebrants Arrive - 17
4. Anais Nin: Life as Celebration - 27
5. Frances Steloff: Reminisces on the Gotham Book Mart - 33
6. William Claire: The Relevance of Literary Magazines - 47
7. Evelyn J. Hinz: The Creative Critic - 57
8. Daisy Aldan: Books Created by the Living Hand - 66
9. Anais Nin: Excerpts from the **Diary** - 77
10. Beatrice Harris: Difficulties of Being Woman & Artist - 85
11. Anna Balakian: The Poetic Reality of Anais Nin - 91
12. Presentations by Celebrants - 107

Part III:
Outward from the Dream

13. Letters & Things - 119
14. Larry Sheehan: I Celebrate Therefore I Am - 124
15. Anais Nin: The Magic Circles Weekend - 142

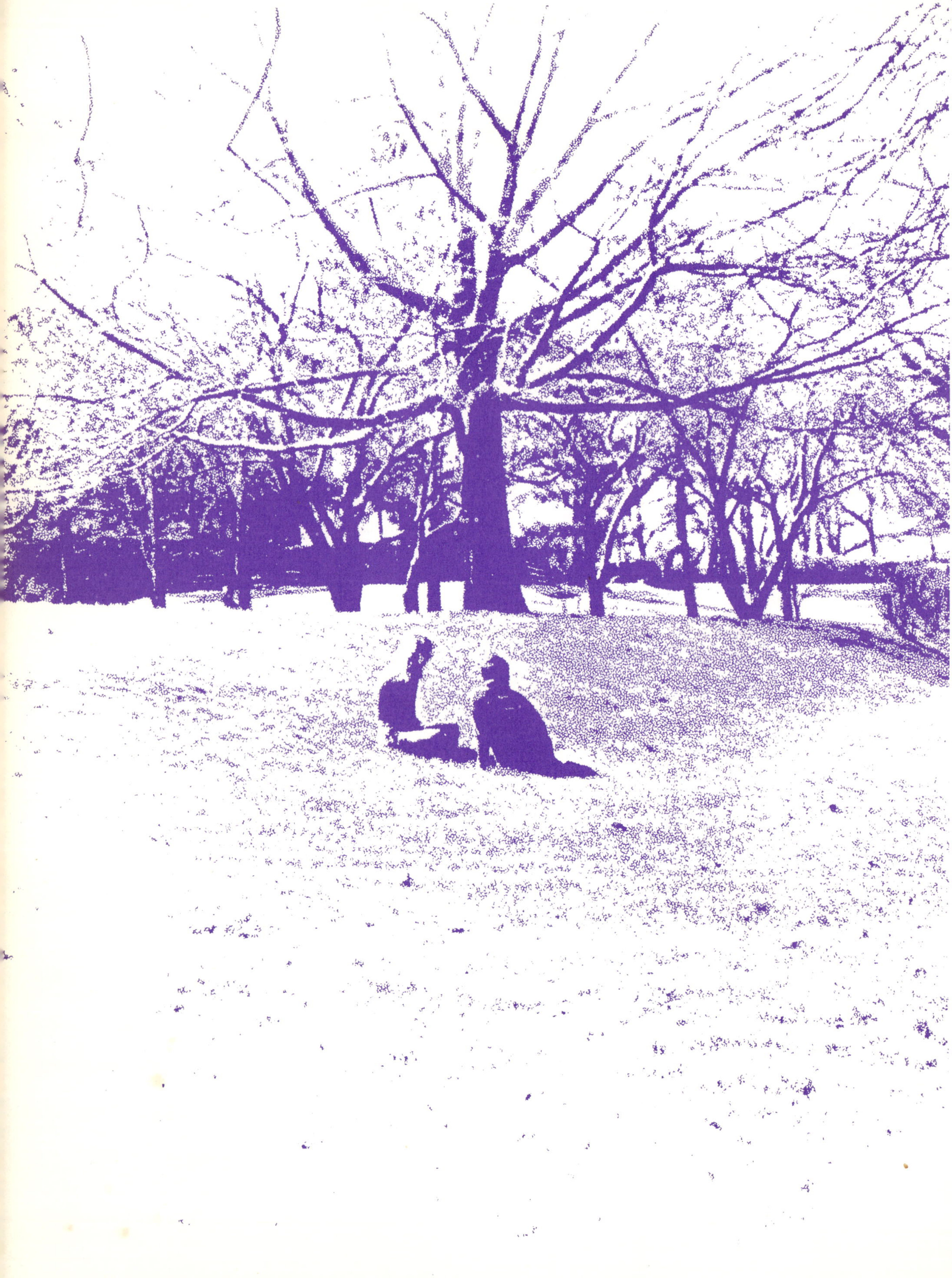

PREFACE

Women Reconstructing the World

"Nothing endures," said Varda, "unless it has first been transposed into a myth."—Because a myth is the embodiment of some unchanging aspect of human nature; it is a sort of x-ray vision of what lies beneath the costuming of the present, a kind of cosmic camera by which the haze of history is brought into definite focus. Anais, however, best expresses the idea in the third Volume of her **Diary** when she observed that It is always the same story one is telling. But from a different angle. The story is the myth, the angle is history—the sequential record of the many ways in which the story has been told.

The thought occurred to me as I participated in the weekend events at Wainwright House and when I recollected my impressions later of whether or not the gathering at Rye was a mythic one in this sense, and if so what was its prototype. That is, to borrow Nin's terminology, I began to wonder whether the attitudes expressed by the participants during the course of the three days were relatively unprecedented or whether they were simply the new angle from which an old story was being told.

There were men present at the gathering and the purpose of the weekend I believe was to celebrate and encourage artistic achievement and creative aspiration in general. But the majority of the participants were women and the emphasis seemed to be upon the artist, she. The story told within this narrowed frame of reference it seemed to me had as its theme both the need for a change with respect to the general attitude toward woman's creative role and the changes that had been wrought as evidenced by the art on display and the narratives of success and determination.

In that the tenor of this theme was thus the progress that had been made and the necessity for liberation from the past the spirit of the gathering was explicitly anti-mythic; the feeling generated was that this gathering signaled and epitomized a new age; the implicit and explicit argument was that what was being experienced was not a contemporary expression of a recurring phenomena but on the contrary a unique moment in history.

Yet the more I thought about it the more I began to wonder whether this spirit and feeling itself did not have precedents, and I thought about it the more because, according to Varda's statement, if the situation were not mythic then its significance would not be an enduring one, and as a participant I did not want to think that I had been a part of something that was ephemeral. So I took the liberty and recourse of generalizing the spirit of liberation I encountered into a theme of woman's rebellion against man and the place she had been assigned in the cosmic scheme. Thus the question now became one of whether ever before a woman had asserted her independence and proved it. Was there a mythological prototype for the woman who proclaimed her self-sufficiency and refused to blindly accept the demands of her mate or of a male code; did ancient history include the tale of a woman who found and established her identity in terms of her relationships not with the opposite but with those of her own sex?

I thought of Eve, who if in plucking that apple disobeyed God had in the first place gone against Adam's injunction by going to the site of the forbidden tree alone; I thought of Psyche, who rebelled against her lover's command that she should blindly accept him without asking questions by lighting a candle and looking at him one night after he had come to her and lay sleeping; and I thought of Sappho, of her love poems, and of her Lesbian isle.

In spirit, certainly these great women constituted the advance guard of the militancy and victory expressed at Rye. The same story then was being retold; but not only had the angle changed, however, the conclusion also stuck a different note. For whereas as a result of her liberation Eve lost Paradise, and Psyche her lover, and Sappho her life, the women at Rye protested their success and happiness. Tears not of regret but of triumphant elation overwhelmed one's eyes, as one listened to the protestations of elation instead of regret that concluded the individual narratives of rebellion. Lady Macbeth did not protest her innocence half so effectively as the many female participants protested their happiness.

So ultimately my impressions of the weekend at Wainwright house leave me swinging between the boughs of a paradox. I am intuitively a believer in the archetypal creed of **eadem, sed aliter,** but to practice such a faith one must deny the direction spearheaded by the gathering at Rye. When Varda entitled one of his collages "Women Reconstructing the World,' he was according to his own definition of enduring art evoking a prototype; was the program of liberation outlined one late April weekend similarly archetypal?

Evelyn J. Hinz,
Post Doctoral Fellow,
University of Manitoba,
Winnipeg, Canada.

PART I:

Circles & Dreams

CHAPTER ONE
THE COSMOS OF ANAIS NIN

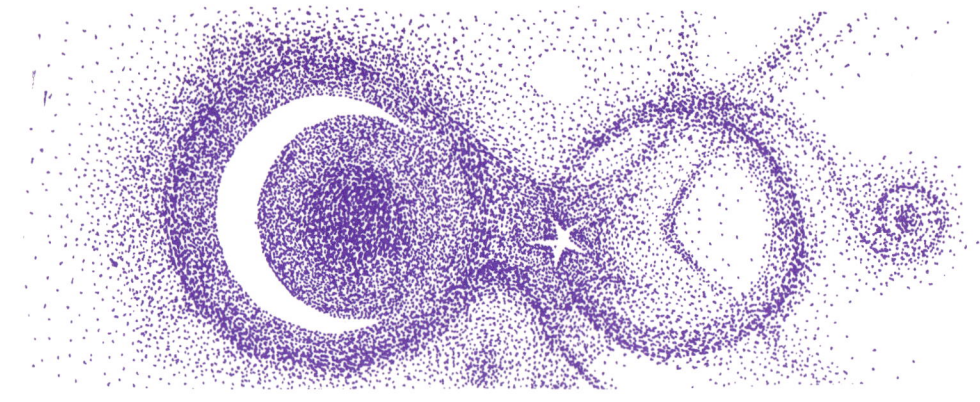

*September 1972. I see and speak to Anais Nin for the first time at a party in the Gotham Book Mart Gallery, given upon the publication of Volume IV of her **Diary**. The room is packed with people, many strangers to each other, but the intersection of our lives at that moment seems magical, in retrospect. Frances Steloff, the eighty-four year old mother of the Gotham Book Mart, is there, busily tending to everyone's needs. So is Donna Ippolito, young editor from Swallow Press, which then is considering a manuscript of mine about the consciousness-raising of women artists, called **UNMASKING: Ten Women in Metamorphosis.** Since Swallow Press published Nin's novels, I feel that if Swallow publishes mine (they do), I would share a bond with her.*

*Also present is my close artist friend, Adele Aldridge. We had met when we joined a group of feminist artists at the same time. When this group had encouraged me to write more about myself and I resisted, thinking that form was not "good" enough, Adele gave me the **Diaries of Anais Nin** to read, which revolutionized my aesthetic theories and style of life. Adele had long felt dedicated to Nin, and we shared many deep discussions about her life and work.*

*After an exchange of letters, Anais Nin invites me to visit her. The opportunity seems like a dream come true, which I want to share with Adele, so I bring her with me. First, Adele asks the **I Ching** what Anais will think of us, and receives the hexagram of the creative heaven over the clinging fire, signifying fellowship. That appears to be true, as the intertwining circles of our dreams unfold.*

Anais is composed. She is a slender, strong-stemmed woman with coppery hair swept up in the back and vivid, round, blue eyes. Her eyes search and welcome us. Her skin is smooth and powdered; her lips deep rose. She wears a long black dress and purple shoes. On her wrist is a watch with wide, leather band. Anais Nin, the woman of many selves, is called "Scheherazade of the Twentieth Century".

This woman, who in her late twenties and full of fears and doubts about herself, wore costumes in public. Living in Louvesciennes, France, at the time outwardly tranquil, pleasant, orderly, but inwardly chaotic, impassioned, troubled, she put on disguises to create new personages for herself, to escape, and ward off her enemies. With the publication of her first book, **D.H. Lawrence: An Unprofessional Study,** *she made more frequent trips to Paris, became involved with June and Henry Miller, psychoanalysts Allendy and Otto Rank, who restored her strength by setting her free in new worlds. Then she made a conscious effort to strip herself of frivolity, luxury, pleasures by depriving herself of desired objects, giving away her money, living humbly and resourcefully to be close to her friends and allies, the artists and writers. Her dress reflected the change, became simpler, yet never lost its subtle drama. There were always to be the capes, artful dresses, symbolic colors.*

Anais shades the blinds for our talk. Instantly the room becomes a private sanctuary of warm glows and mysterious shadows. I think of all the dense atmospheres Anais has created, as told in her **Diaries.** *The house in Louvesciennes with its red room for vehemence, blue for dreaming, grey for working, peach for gentleness. Its earthiness. Geraniums in the window. A fountain. Then a houseboat on the Seine. The many apartments with simple furniture but always something unique, such as the astrological charts of Conrad Moricand, the old table carved and painted by artist friends. About beds she wrote:*

> ... Another bed which was an aphrodisiac was the Bohemian mattress on the floor. Escaping from the elevation seemed also to bring one closer to the earth, to flesh, and there was no fear of rolling away from the bed, falling. It suggested a lair, closer to primitive life, Oriental life, closer to the senses, travel and camping in the deserts, closer to human and animal nature. It reminded me of Fatima in Morocco, of harems, tents of **A Thousand and One Nights . . .**"

Anais Nin through her clothes, dwellings, travels, friends, and books always created her world to counter the poisons she saw on a large scale outside, believing that the revolution had to take place first within oneself in order to change the world. We recognize that we are engaged in the same battle and that she has expressed our own conflicts and aspirations in her books; by unmasking her innermost convictions, no matter how vulnerable she became, she attained universality. She has been equally courageous in carving out her place in the world of literature. Life as she lived it and created it in her books is a heroic adventure of our time.

"Anais" is a Greek name that was fashionable at the time she was born. As a child, in France she was accustomed to living among musicians, artists, intellectuals, and aristocrats. She recalls that she was always reading, even the books on top of her father's shelves. At the age of eleven her parents separated and she, with her two brothers, was brought to America by her mother for a new and difficult life. Here Anais attended public schools but left at high school, developing her reading and writing on her own. An English teacher had advised her to write more colloquially, but Anais flowered as an international writer with roots in surrealism, ancient and modern literature, psychology, and music. Her speech retains an international character as well. She speaks precise English with a French accent. Her voice is soft, low-key. Although she is quick to laugh, she seems easily susceptible to dark thoughts. A flicker in her eyes and shadow passes through the joy. She says though that she is in harmony with her life now.

Like Eurydice she descended alone into the dark labyrinthian depths of the underground, only in her case the depths were the womb-cells of the mind, the unconscious. Bravely crossing new barriers, she explored the interior landscape - its mountains, valleys, oceans, jungles, frigid and torrid zones - and, as with the galaxies, found no end to it. She wrote, Living is the constant motion towards unraveling a dynamic movement from mystery to mystery. Her goal was self-discovery, the mastery of her destiny.

She knew equally well states of heightened joy, inspired by the imagination or art, and massive despair, crash landings. Fearing fragmentation, as in looking at the self in a shattered mirror, and the stale binding structure of society's religious, cultural, and racial attitudes, she sought wholeness of personality. This odyssey is documented in the **Diaries.** *Not one man, but many loves and friendships went into her quest. Relationships were not enough; there was always the need to write and to create. As she set forth on her voyage a solitary and independent woman, from the experience of having given birth to a dead child, her way was marked with danger. But, in the course of her explorations into the interior, she was to achieve nothing less than the creation of herself.*

For her guide she used psychoanalysis. She recalls when she was considering publishing Volume I of the **Diaries,** *how she had a dream in which she opened her front door and fatal radiation overcame her. Symbolically to her the radiation meant her fears of exposure to the outside world, which was to become an ever present fact in her life, just as strontium 90 penetrates and stays with the body. The dream represented her fear of the world, the fear of judgment, the fear of not being loved, the fear of having everyone say, 'This is a monster'.*

Psychoanalysis liberated her from destructive fears and guilts inherited from parents, Catholicism, men, politics. She used it to meet the crises in her life, but she also turned from it for nourishment to more submarine regions of the imagination. To her, psychoanalysis was limited by its arid objectivity. She eventually transcended her needs for it.

But in her books Anais uses her psychological knowledge and symbols to reveal her characters and their states of being. She practices archaeology of the soul, her purpose being to write dramas as the unconscious lives them. In **Spy in the House of Love,** *the psycho-drama is about a woman who feels compelled to leave a placid relationship with her husband for many other loves and feels pursued by guilt. In* **Ladders to Fire,** *she portrays a group of people who attempt to find lovers in men and women to fulfill various emotional needs. Like an analyst she constructs character from fragments that distinguish between his/her fantasy and reality. Thus Sabina is a feverish, restless woman who wears red and silver and is associated with the sound and sight of fire engines. Sabina's behavior vacillates between impulsiveness and guilt. Believing that analytical insight wrapped in poetry was far more potent than bare analysis, Anais described neurosis, people with broken connections, diffused visions, who enact symbolic dramas. The characters who can relentlessly examine their natures are shown restored to their full human lives. By thus presenting humanism, the value of her literature, Anais hoped, would destroy the seeds of war and prejudice.*

Anais keeps the rare first editions of her books in a large transparent box. Precious works of art, all of them. The hand-set volumes of **Under A Glass Bell** *and* **Winter of Artifice** *contain beautiful type, set straight for narrative, in italics for reveries, on heavy stock paper with engravings by Ian Hugo.*

Anais spent six months setting the type by hand for **Under A Glass Bell.** *What propelled her to painstakingly learn the techniques of printing, scrounge around for a foot-treadle press, and spend months of hard, physical labor printing her own books? The power of the dream. She always believed in what she was writing. Already in France she had published the book on D.H. Lawrence and* **House of Incest.** *She was not to be defeated because the publishing establishment in America didn't accept her at that time. The volumes which she did print turned out to be exceptionally beautiful and sold out immediately at the Gotham Book Mart. She continued to write more novels and articles, becoming well known in underground circles. Her persistence, despite opposition for many years, took the courage that is so admired today by the do-it-yourself, "consciousness III" people.*

Her perseverance in her work comes from an obsession to weave a connection with the world. On the one hand, this means that her writing itself brings her friends and new worlds, as publishing the critical study of D.H. Lawrence resulted in her meeting Henry Miller, who introduced her to the vibrant life of Paris streets, and **House of Incest** *brought her the Durrells. Her books are* passports out of loneliness. *On the other hand, she writes to preserve experience, to give back to the world some of the joy and beauty she took out of it. She also writes to dispel feelings of loss, from being uprooted, destruction and death. She writes before her memory can distort experience, desiring to recreate the feelings of life in all their spontaneity.*

A close relationship exists between her **Diaries,** *novels, and critical works. The* **Diaries,** *her "laboratory", capture the immediate flow of her experiences. The novels are more consciously formal, containing much material "distilled" from the* **Diaries.** *The critical works explain her innovative literary theories in depth. She favors the content of the* **Diaries,** *finding them closer to the courses of true feeling.* Too much awareness without accompanying experience is a skeleton without the flesh of life. *She always writes in the* language *of emotion and the senses, which is different from that of the intellect.*

Reading the novels is often like reading poetry in prose. Complex, sensuous rhythms and imagery are set up. Structure is often symphonic. Objects are symbolic. All work toward a larger revelation of characters in their relationships. Anais presents her characters at the heightened moment when people reveal themselves most fully. She dwells on essences, rather than outward manifestations of character. She tries to show her characters as they act, reflect, feel and suffer simultaneously. Leaving out what does not contribute, she lets the form of her writing erupt by itself from the inner direction. She does not try to fit her work into any literary mold; she has used her ideas and artistry to produce an innovative body of literature.

Even though Henry Miller had opposed Anais' writing the diaries (as had Allendy and Rank), she feels that because she was challenged by him to defend herself, he had a beneficial influence on her. But wasn't she more considerate and stimulating to the creativity of Miller, for instance, than he was to her? She answers that he didn't understand women and knowing how he distorted real persons in his fiction, she asked him not to write about her. Her most satisfying relationships have always been with artists and students because they are more interested in the personal and more accepting of women's expansion. Europeans, she thinks, are more understanding than Americans; the latter have been done-in by Puritanism.

Just as friction is what makes the pearl of an oyster, so the pain in her relationship with her father started Anais on her famous **Diary.** *And, despite her attitude toward her father's criticisms of her, his fickleness for women, his unfair solicitations of her as an adult, she gave him love, sympathy and attention when he asked for it. For the sake of intimate communion with others she was to follow the same pattern with June, Gonzalo, Frances, Robert and others. Silencing her thoughts, she praised the incorrigibly lazy Gonzalo's capacity to enjoy life, let him burn her books, gave Miller her typewriter, Robert Duncan her bottom dollar. Sometimes the sacrifices literally made her ill. She would fear that her work was being destroyed. She often wondered how some of her friends could be so cruel to her, but she never turned against them. She knew how to feel personally responsible for others in a cold and often inhuman world.* If all of us acted in unison as I act individually there would be no wars and no poverty.

Although Anais used familiar people in her novels, she maintains that her writing is not autobiographical. Readers of the stories and novels can find her maid in "The Mouse", Conrad Moricand as "The Mohican", Jean Carteret in the "The All-Seeing", June Miller as Sabina in **House of Incest** *and* **Spy in the House of Love,** *but know that these people have been "alchemized" by the quality of Anais' writing. When Anais uses her own experiences for material, such as in the story "Houseboat" or "My Own Labyrinth", her objective is to poetically evaluate the emotions involved and attain a universal meaning, which is the highest form of objectivity. This relation between life and art is expressed perfectly in her preface to* **House of Incest:**

> This morning I got up to begin this book I coughed. Something was coming out of my throat: it was strangling me. I broke the thread which held it and yanked it out. I went back to bed and said: I have just spat out my heart. There is an instrument called the quena made of human bones. It owes its origin to the worship of an Indian for his mistress. When she died he made a flute out of her bones. The quena has a more penetrating, more haunting sound than the ordinary flute. Those who write know the process. I thought of it as I was spitting out my heart.
> Only I do not wait for my love to die.

Suddenly the aroma of burning coffee fills the air, and it seems strange to watch Anais hurry out to tend to it. Actually for all her adventuresome life she has never been freed from domestic duties. Unlike Henry Miller who would work non-stop on his writing if the mood seized him, she only had a few times in her life when she could devote up to four straight days to uninterrupted writing. A big difference between most men and women, Anais believes, is that a man will leave a woman for the sake of his work, but a woman will leave her work for the man. She describes how two writers whom she knew married, and the husband immediately insisted upon having a studio outside the house, leaving the wife to work in the home with the hubbub of the house, guests and children.

One of the most important forces infusing Anais' work is her desire to speak for all women. She thinks that men are fearful of exploring women, and women fearful of saying what they feel. Applying this to the male literary critic when he reviews the books of women writers, the male appears to focus unduly on sexual encounters, to make moralistic judgments and useless personal comments rather than offer an interpretation of the work and an appreciation of its literary mode. A certain jealousy distorts the vision.

To Anais, woman is the grand lover of the world. Woman represents creativity and union, the physical and spiritual link between unconscious and the objective. Man is too abstract, because he denies the personal roots of all his thought. Women need to find a sensitive balance with man to meet the problems of the world. They need to find more ways to relate to the cosmos than just as the universal Mother and Priestess-Prostitute.

In her writing Anais desires to express the drama of woman in relation to herself, her conflict between selfishness and individuality, and how to make manifest the cosmic consciousness she feels. *In the novels she creates an archetypal heroine through the use of four major woman characters. Briefly, Anais writes that Djuna is to represent perception, Stella the blind and suffering, Sabina the free woman, Lillian one who seeks liberation in aggression. Moreover, as Evelyn Hinz writes in* **The Mirror and the Garden,** *in addition to elaborating on this collective heroine, Anais sees* woman as more elemental than man, *and since it is the restrictions civilization imposes upon natural man and the consequences which concern Anais,* the female figure is a poetically necessary vehicle.

Anais avoids the explicit use of sex, although her writing is heavy with sensuality and love. To her mind D.H. Lawrence began using the language of sex but she takes us further into the feelings of woman's sexual ecstasy, hunger, jealousy and guilt. Love in her books is freely bestowed, a fact that went long unperceived perhaps because she has been too daring in revealing the truth.

Today Anais is carrying on a long, marvelous dialogue with the world. Thousands of letters, many of them long and confessional, have poured in over the years. She is happy about the attention her work is receiving and gives her time generously to lectures, readings and visits with admirers.

Anais Nin combines Old World European and New World American values. Cherishing the civilized mores, art and beauty of all cultures, she also loves action and adventure. Especially she cultivates the arts of introspection and friendship.

She has no yen to be rich, makes no distinction among classes or races of people. She is sensitive to the individual and how he/she is symptomatic of the whole world. She doesn't drink, prefers the use of imagination to drugs, accepts the poetry of astrology. Many men and women have considered her decades ahead of her time in articulating the world we live in.

Many people, too, have found in her personal relationships, hard work and struggle to write, the reassurance that things can be done that way. "Unblocking" people is part of her power. Women who see in her a reflection of themselves, concern for the same problems and fears, feel a new freedom to develop their gifts. She creates a climate of intimacy wherein persons can expand themselves anew.

In the novels Anais has presented us with a composite woman, a portrait of the feminine archetype that sprang from the visions she had from going down into the unconscious self and bringing them back to life. In the **Diaries** *the heroic voyager is Anais, struggling to turn destructive forces into constructive ones. She has always felt that to counter the poisons of impotent, passive despair in the world, a cosmic consciousness which solved dualities and divisions was needed. Through the intensive examination of her biological and psychic impulses, an unmasking of her human self, she revealed these cosmic truths, with which both male and female identify. She achieved universal understanding and communication.*

Woman, *Anais wrote,* is the mermaid with fish-tail dipped in the unconscious. *So Anais, born Pisces, seems like the creator-goddess of Sumerian myth, Tiamat, who appeared out of the sea as a flesh-and-blood woman to instruct people in all things that tended to soften manners and humanize their lives.*

She concludes our visit with an embrace.

CHAPTER TWO

MAGIC CIRCLES

November. A purple invitation arrives in the mail, announcing a university weekend for Anais Nin at Berkeley, California. I am miserable because I cannot go. I say, "WHY DON'T WE DO ONE HERE?"

Adele answers, "YES, WHY DON'T WE?"

Neither one of us knows whether we can really swim in these new waters or not. We are both hard at our own art work, trying to achieve financial independence, and caring for a family. But we decide to jump in anyway.

Our ideas take shape. We don't want thousands of people, as were at Berkeley, but an intimate group in a comfortable atmosphere, where conversation and revelation can flow easily. Knowing Anais, we feel privacy is a must. There is a place called Wainwright House located in Rye, New York on the Long Island Sound. It is a mansion where weekends of a philosophical or spiritual nature are given regularly for small groups. We could sleep and eat meals there. For an entire weekend we would be able to withdraw from the outside world. It seems a perfect setting. My husband, Larry, offers to be our assistant, but he worries what the people who come will find to talk about.

"Don't worry", Adele says, "We won't be able to stop them".

We want the weekend to profoundly influence the creative lives of the people who choose to participate. In its design, which involves as much selection and decision making as a work of art, we see it as a new form of education as well as a gift from us to Anais Nin. We decide to call our project "Magic Circles", because of its many meanings for us. First, the magical effect Nin's writing has on us. Then, we hope that the people who come will intersect with each other, return to their worlds, radiating their new awarenesses in ever expanding concentric circles. Also, magic circle means mandala, which is an archetypal symbol of the soul's integration. It is a motif which Adele has explored in a long series of paintings.

Throughout January and February we enjoy the fun-work of making plans and contacting people for the program. Anais Nin is the center of this magic circle, within which we discern the life motions of Frances Steloff and her long supportive friendship with Anais. We think of Anna Balakian, professor of French and Comparative Literature and critic of the Surrealist and Symbolist Movements in Literature, which Anais knew well. Balakian had also written excellent reviews of Nin's work in "The New York Times." Seeking someone who had taken the trouble to make and print beautiful books with her own hands, as Nin did in the early days of her career, we discover the poet Daisy Aldan, long a friend of Nin's. We also invite William Claire, because of his knowledge of literary magazines and because Nin was on the advisory board of his "Voyages". Evelyn Hinz we ask because of her critical study of the complete works of Nin in **The Mirror and the Garden.** *And finally since we want to have a discussion of the special psychological problems involved in being a woman and artist, Anais introduces us to Dr. Beatrice Harris, a psychologist. Later on, we discover circles within this circle. For instance, Daisy Aldan worked on a doctorate on Surrealism under the guidance of Anna Balakian and everyone knows Frances Steloff in some way, either as a friend or seller of books.*

When we visit Daisy Aldan about her part in the program, she prophetically says, Everything happens for a reason. There are no accidents. Everything is coming together for a purpose.

We write a lot of letters and make many phone calls and trips. Anais keeps helpfully in touch and corresponds frequently on purple cards emblazoned with a Pisces symbol. A special, unconscious affinity with Frances Steloff amazes us and continues to do so. The first time we see her is at a lecture on Symbolism at the Gotham Book Mart. Her cat sits on Adele's lap. The very next day Adele and I are at an Intensive Journal Weekend with depth psychologist Ira Progoff. We are concentrating on our writing. Completely unaware of each other, Adele and I are writing dialogues, using Frances as a wisdom figure.

> A tiny white-haired lady tip toes into the room. No one notices her because we are all in a dreamy state, meditating and writing. I look up and go back to my writing. POW! That little old lady flowing beside me is Frances Steloff. Where am I? Am I fantasizing? Awake? Asleep? I explain to Progoff what has happened and how my fantasies are intermingling with reality. He laughs and nods in understanding and says, "Oh, that happens to me all the time. Think nothing of it and continue what you were doing." THINK NOTHING OF IT, he says with cool.*

---

*From Adele's **Dream Log,** *her personal account of the weekend, the source of all quotations by Adele used in this book.*

We literally vibrate with excitement in describing this event to Frances who enjoys it thoroughly.

One night Anais Nin is to read at the Poetry Center and we have dinner with Frances beforehand. We follow her, as she leads us hurriedly to a Japanese restaurant, where she knows we can get good vegetables. She is preoccupied with her responsibility for operating the book table at the Poetry Center. We try to make her understand her important role in the Weekend Celebration, but she does not really believe us then.

At the Poetry Center we help her unload books and set up the table, Anais sweeps by us, smiling warmly. Frances, Adele, Larry, and I listen to the reading. Future participants of our Weekend are in the audience but we don't know them yet. Larry helps us pass out a circular which says,

If You Are Interested In Spending A Weekend With ANAIS NIN Contact MAGIC CIRCLES

Another day we view the films of Ian Hugo. The man - an engraver, filmmaker, and businessman - is charming, intense and friendly. His films are like dreams of color and movement. Adele says, **he has said what all painters try to say but can only succeed at in the mind's eye.** *We are borne away in the flow of images appearing in the dark and afterwards are reluctant to leave. Out of these marvelous flights via film we select with difficulty three for the program. We choose his biographical one and two with glimpses of Anais.*

March. Adele and I make a brochure which crystallizes the whole event. We send out a big mailing and hold our breaths about whether others feel the power of the magic too. Surprising letters come in from Ohio, Illinois, Wisconsin, California, Texas, Virginia, Massachusetts, New York, Washington, and Connecticut!

> ... YES! YES! YES!
> I CAN COME.
> (PRAISE BE THE POWERS
> THAT BE,
> AND BANKS ...)
>
> —Bebe Herring

> ... I should very much like to join you for the Weekend with Anais Nin. I am a professor of French Literature at the University of Massachusetts with a special interest in 19th and 20th century literature and women writers in France, England, and the United States. I have started to work on a study of intimate writings - diary, personal, memoirs, autobiography - that includes the *Diaries of Anais Nin*.
>
> - Elaine Marks

A person unknown to us, named Lynne Honickman, who cannot attend herself, sends a check so that "two others who cannot afford the monetary might have the opportunity/luxury to participate - meet with the labyrinthian wonder of this extraordinary human being."

One young girl sends her response on a Jasmine soap wrapper from India. It comes folded in a tiny square, wrapped in orange tissue, and sealed with wax.

Another sends a hand-lettered broadsheet quoting Shakespeare. One letter is delicately water-colored.

A college boy writes frequent semi-poetic letters in a thin, tall, Gothic print with his rapidograph pen. He says his brother is coming from San Francisco expressly for this Weekend. In the ensuing days he also telephones several times, always trying to find out more about us and Nin.

The gay originality of these letters tells us a lot about the people who want to come to our Weekend.

Part II: April 28-30th.

The Living Dream Weekend!

CHAPTER THREE

The Celebrants Arrive

Friday dusk April 28. The moment has come. This evening, Adele notes, we are to have a full moon which represents the energy of things brought to fruition. As the people arrive at Wainwright House we begin to realize that many have come out of a semi-conscious need to be with Anais at this particular juncture in their lives. There is a shared hunger that has made them trek here from far corners of the United States.

Many person's lives intertwine in ways that astonish us. For instance, Adele has planned with whom individuals would share a room. Her intuition is praised several times. During the champagne reception she is told by May Garelick, an author of many books for children, that she is rooming with a niece, Elaine Marks, whom she didn't even know was coming. After further conversation, Adele realizes that May is also a friend of her mother-in-law's, an artist who had lived in Paris many years. Also our feminist artist friends are put together in a separate carriage house of their own, where they are grateful for the privacy that permits many deep conversations to flourish well into the night. Trew Bennett, a potter from Virginia, and Moira Collins from Illinois share a room and have an intense feeling that, although unknown by name to another, they've been friends for a long time.

And so it goes during the reception, as slides of John Pearson's photographs from his book, **Kiss The Joy as it Flies,** *Adele's prints from her book on the* **I Ching** *flash in counterpoint to the conversation, little by little setting the mood for the drama about to unfold. Bebe Herring, very young, enters the solarium. A painter named Joan Anacreon thinks,*

> I am delighted with the sight of a young woman with glorious long dark hair, sitting in a marvelous rattan chair that encircled her and regally frames her beauty. She wears a long black dress, and a graceful glowing red shawl carelessly spills from her side down to the floor. Her name is Bebe, and she is a painting!

Right from the beginning people talk to each other with a marked absence of formality and introduction. Georgiana Peacher, an older woman who had attended the event in California earlier that year, is quiet and modest. Everyone is stunned about her undertaking the silk-screening of a novel. My husband brings in from New York Daisy Aldan and Frances Steloff with her shopping bags of books. A table soon overflows with Anais' works and Daisy Aldan's.

Paintings, sculpture, fantastic capes and masks, pottery are on exhibit. There is great diversity but a unified spirit permeates everything.

Anais arrives finally with the psychologist, Beatrice Harris. Both women are cloaked. After refreshing in her room, Anais comes down the stairs and into the solarium. Her presence is felt everywhere instantly. She is like the sun, giving light and warmth and nourishment to people, enticing their creative selves to unfold, like flowers in bloom. Throughout the Weekend I observe her listening to others, embracing them, constantly attentive.

> Trew Bennett:* ... I am going to the Celebration! I feel self-conscious and somehow embarrassed by my excitement and thrill ... We arrive at Wainwright House, a huge and imposing mansion, overlooking the Sound. Valerie meets me and asks me to arrange my pottery on a front table. I enter the room of people-sounds and find signs of other artist's work. I see Anais Nin, and she carefully remembers who I am from my letters. She has delicate, slim fingers and a lovely, smiling natural shyness, a dedication to inner beauty and expression. Later that evening I say something to her about all the interlocking circles here. She responds, leans forward, and kisses me on the cheek. Her soft French accent gives a sweet richness to her, and she appears like a little girl at times. Her strength is in her vulnerability, - she has the gift of great openness and this she also inspires. I sense though that she is equally private, and that she maintains this privacy in a most artful, elusive, and womanly way ... There is a certain breed of people here this weekend, women who have a similar blood type running through their veins.
>
> Nadine Daily:* ... I arrive. The welcome warm gestures, busy organization, my room to freshen. How I wished to lie still, I did not wish too much. Nourishment came as I looked out the white muslin window to that tree at ochered yellow sunset silhouetted.

Dinner is light, sparkling with bright anticipation. So, afterwards, is the mood as we gather in the library. Adele and I have decided that we should all take a turn at introducing ourselves briefly. With quaking heart I begin by telling the story about how I met Anais Nin.

*This and all following quotations are from her Journal.

*Also from her Journal.

19

> **Adele follows tremulously:** My first awareness of Anais dates back when my ex-mother-in-law, an artist, lived in Paris in the thirties and knew Henry Miller but never had a friendship with Anais. She used to reminisce about Paris and say, 'There was this woman that Henry used to talk about, named Anais Nin. They were very serious but he would never introduce her, keeping her on a distant pedestal.' I always remembered that, but since I had never heard of Nin, I didn't know what she was talking about. Years went by and then I read the letters of Lawrence Durrell to Henry Miller, in which he mentions Anais. So when the first *Diary* came, I pounced on it and was overwhelmed. I also wrote letters to Nin which, significantly, I never mailed. When I was a child I had no model with whom to identify. I grew up under very ordinary conditions and always felt crazy because what I was never went along with what I saw around me in society. In the *Diary* I felt identification with Nin in a different realm. For instance, when I was reading the third *Diary*, I wanted to print a book by hand, the *I Ching* book. I had no convictions that it was worth doing, because nobody asked or wanted me to do it, but the *Diary* taught me that if you don't passionately believe in yourself, no one else does. I consider that an extremely important event in my life. Also the *Diaries* enabled me to live out fantasies and this weekend is one of them.

Frances Steloff has been straining to hear every word that is said. Now she speaks in her own firm voice, making everyone laugh over her modesty and practical business sense:

> Frances: My first attention was called to Anais when I got a letter back in 1939 during the War, which said, 'We all in Paris on the Left Bank know about The Gotham Book Mart. I have some books that I would like to send which you can sell for me and someday I hope to get to New York.' And she said that she didn't want them bombed. I was terribly pleased to think that anyone in Paris on the Left Bank knew about the Gotham Book Mart. So I said, 'Yes, of course we'll do our best to sell your books.' I have felt very guilty all these years thinking that I sold these books at $1.00! First editions of *D.H. Lawrence: An Unprofessional Study!* Well, by the time I sold them all, I would have paid $25.00 each to get them back. I didn't realize that this was one of the best studies of D.H. Lawrence that has ever been published. So we corresponded until I think 1940 when Anais came and the rest of that story is in the *Diary*.

Anais: Frances Steloff had the only book shop in New York, we were told, where you could browse and where you were not forced to buy a book. You could almost read the book standing up. We knew her as owner of a warm welcoming bookshop like Sylvia Beach's.

> Frances: Anais was always so thoughtful and kind and appreciative that she just drew the very best out of everyone.

Kitty Penner: I'm a painter and one of the Connecticut Feminists in the Arts.

Elaine Streitfeld: (emotionally) Driving all the way here I was crying for joy. The thought that keeps coming up in everyone's conversation is, 'I have to **believe in myself,** I have to **find myself,** I have to **express myself** and **develop myself.'** I feel that this weekend is going to be a turning point in my life and that many of you feel this way. **We want our souls to be expressed and we want to be like the dream.** I hope I can become what I think is inside of me and I hope that it happens to all of you.

Sas Colby: I'm an artist and work mostly in fabric. I made the capes and fantasy masks here.

Suzanne Benton: I'm a metal sculptor. I had heard about Anais Nin but I hadn't read anything of hers. Even so she represented a world that I wanted and the woman's journey, which certainly as a woman I wanted as my journey.

Evelyn Clark: I am a feminist and a revolutionary political person. At a very low point in my life, the **Diary** *gave me something to hold onto. Later, my feminist group decided to invite Anais to speak publicly in Boston. That weekend we interviewed Anais also and published the interview in our feminist magazine, "The Second Wave."*

Nancy Williamson: I write and I'm a good friend of Evelyn's. One day Evelyn told me that I should read these **Diaries.** I had always read diaries but they were men's - like Camus and Gide, yet I had always kept diaries. When I read the **Diary of Anais Nin** I was extremely moved like the rest of you were.

Daisy Aldan: Poetry is the core around which my other activities center. I also publish books and I teach creative writing at the New York School of Art and Science. In 1953 I was a rather young outcast teacher, the one whom all of the other teachers gossiped about in school. I introduced a creative writing course and one of my students brought me a copy of Anais' **House of Incest,** *a first edition. He said, 'I think you'll be interested in this.' I opened that book and almost fainted. First of all it had so much to do with my doctorate on "The Influence of French Surrealism on American Literature" and also it contained fantastic poetry in prose. Then I found out that Anais had done a book of short stories called* **Under a Glass Bell** *which I started teaching to my creative writing class. I was almost thrown out of school for this innovation. I never told Anais this. Then I wrote to Anais for an interview and found the most beautiful woman I had ever seen, as well as very gracious and generous. She gave me copies of all her books, and I stayed up all night long reading them. I continued introducing her work to my students. I heard her read at the Poetry Center and watched her sell her own books at the counter.*

When I started putting out a magazine called **Folder** *and sent her a copy, she wrote me a letter and said, 'What ever happened to you? Here I gave you all my books and never heard from you again.' We started a little correspondence in which I told her I was teaching her stories to my classes. She was in despair at the time, saying that the critics were very unkind and there was a lack of recognition in the commercial world. So I told her that she must go on writing because her writing is so great and beautiful that it will find its way.*

Anais is a tremendous support and inspiration to me in my work. I always felt when she came into New York that some particular light appeared. And when she came to my school to talk to my students, I felt that the walls were falling down. She was a very great inspiration to my students too.

Helen Bidwell: I first read Miss Nin's work in Mr. Claire's magazine "Voyages". I kept talking about Miss Nin so much to Mr. Claire that he said, 'Would you like to try to review one of the diaries?' And so I tried to do the fourth Volume which might be coming out in one of the issues. One idea of hers important to me is that things in the past can be used or worked out in the present.

Caroline Emmet: I go to school in Madison, Wisconsin. I read all of Henry Miller's books and was intrigued by the woman whom he knew and respected. I found a copy of your *Diary* **and it seemed clear that you were my closest friend. I had written diaries since I was about 12, but I never really believed in them. They were for my secrets, my private confessions of hates and miseries. I never held them as valid work so I wrote short stories in the third person, inventing other names for myself and the people I knew. I always thought that that was writing, whereas diaries were an addiction, not to be proud of. When I started reading your** *Diaries* **I began to feel that my own diaries were probably the most solid and real things I had written. Your** *Diaries* **are a goldmine, a really important part of literature that is just beginning to be admired and respected.**

Beatrice Harris: Right now I'm a psychologist: I teach and have a practice. I teach courses that deal with women in terms of their changing roles. I met Anais two years ago when she responded to a letter of mine, and I don't think I can describe all the ways in which her friendship made me grow.

William Claire: I write poems and I'm the editor and publisher of "Voyages," that famous quarterly magazine that hasn't been out in about a year. I first met Miss Nin on a very sad occasion, a memorial service for the late Alan Swallow in New York. Anais was an original advisor - editor of my magazine and any association with her is somewhat like coming into New York and finding fresh air in a very polluted world.

James Mundy: I build pyramids. My foundations are in San Francisco right now, where I've been studying with small presses, printers and poets in the Bay area for about the last year and a half. I am soon to be publishing a book with my brother which I will print in San Francisco.

Trew Bennett: I'm a potter. I first found **Under a Glass Bell** *on a dusty shelf in an antique shop and bought it. I've been in psychoanalysis for a number of years and am aware of the absence of descriptive literature concerning the experience. There are many books that give categories and case histories but it's very hard to find a discussion of the very slow evolutionary process that takes place with all the attendant personal feelings about it.* **The Diaries of Anais Nin,** *especially Volume III, touched on all sorts of personal things for me. I wrote to Anais Nin and she wrote back and I wrote again and she wrote back. I don't know how she had the time to do this!*

Rosalie Gleim: I am a teacher. When I worked on my dissertation, I was allowed to take Anais Nin as a topic. I've always been fascinated by the process of creation, by the process in which people take life and create art out of it and vice versa. People said to me, 'Oh, you are a woman writing about a woman writer.' And I answered, 'I'm not writing about a woman writer. I'm writing about an artist, somebody who has said more about this creative process than anybody I've run across.' People insisted that I write about her as a woman but that was never my point. James Joyce wrote as a man. We don't call him a man artist, we call him an artist. I'd like to discuss this later.

Larry Sheehan: I live at the same address as Valerie. A lot of what I know about Anais Nin I have obtained through the atmosphere that was created by this whole Magic Circle thing. I think it was illustrated best just a week ago when Anais called the house when Valerie wasn't there and I answered the phone and talked to her. Anyway, I was *trying* to talk to her as best I could, with the reputation she had at the other end of the line. In the middle of it - I was already confused - someone started ringing at the door. So I had to excuse myself. I knew that wasn't the right way to handle Miss Nin but I put the phone down and went to the door and it turned out to be a taxi cab driver bearing a telegram from Austin, Texas, from someone who wanted to be sure he could come this weekend! This was something in a long series of small stupefactions that I've experienced in the past year or so!

But I truly do appreciate Anais Nin's work. When I had studied French literature in college I thought that I had pretty much covered the field, but after college I stumbled on some Colette who was never taught there, yet was better than anyone I had ever studied at college. I felt there was and still is a connection between the two women. I think the fact that Anais Nin is being appreciated today by so many people is a revenge in part for Colette's having been blackballed. The only thing I really regret is that Colette had this school friend whose name was Anais, which according to the *Diaries* prevented Anais Nin in the 30's and 40's from ever looking up Colette, because I feel that it would have been a summit meeting of sorts.

And I myself am a writer. I had been employed as an editor and now I've given that up. I'm in the stream now.

> **Anais:** There's an interesting story about Colette that I must tell you about. They wanted to allow her into the French Academy and the judges couldn't question the beauty of her style, but, they said, after all what does she write about, but love, relationships, motherhood, working in a music hall - all ''minor'' themes! But she did get into the Academy.

Lele Krippner: . . . Life is strange. I met Laura Huxley who made a strange remark concerning you and through that remark I started to read your Diary. Then a friend of mine who often comes to Wainwright House sent me a circular about the Magic Circles weekend. My husband gave me this weekend for an anniversary present. So thanks to Laura Huxley and my husband, I'm here.

> **Moira Collins:** I'm a writer and have collected and written commonplace books for a number of years. I was always searching for things that I thought might fit. I saw the *Diaries* one day and all of a sudden it occurred to me that for years I had been trying to pattern my life after men from whose commonplace books I had been collecting and writing. I didn't feel as crazy as perhaps some people thought. I had always hand-done books for my friends with the thought that Henry Miller used to print books for friends which they were delighted to receive. So the *Diaries* to me were personally very important and I started giving them to everyone I knew.

Evelyn Frazier: Professionally I am a social worker, but on my own time I work very hard for the Women's Movement.

> **Lisa Ekstrom:** People say that I'm an artist and I would like to believe that. A couple of years ago my mother and I discovered the *Diaries* and read them and they brought us closer together than we had been before. They also gave me just an incredible feeling of joy and strength to do things that I hadn't thought maybe I could do.

Georgiana Peacher: I started writing some stories when I was 10 years old and that's when I decided I'd be a writer. By the time I was 17 I was quite influenced that this was a very impossible thing for a woman to do. So, completely convinced, I drifted along 30 years, becoming a speech therapist. But I didn't save myself until five years ago when I was in the library looking up some technical texts. I hadn't read any fiction for 30 years because in my field of science we were too busy, but somehow at this time my unconscious mind took me to the fiction department of the library and I went straight for these books - it's very spooky - they were: **House of Incest** *and* **Collages.** *These just changed my life and I went after every book by Anais Nin. Then the* **Diary** *came out, and I discovered a woman who had many feelings that I had but had supressed. I wished I had done everything that I knew I wanted to do when I was 17. So I just decided to do it. I resigned my position and it's exactly five years this month April that I left and started to become a writer full time.*

Elaine Marks: With all due respect I'm a professor of French Literature. I have written a book on Colette and a book on Simone de Beauvoir. For a new book I'm very interested in women diary writers. I've been reading Virginia Woolf's story in manuscript form at the New York Public Library. I just finished reading Anais Nin's *Diary*.

Lele Stephens: I write poems. I was for many years a newspaper columnist but quit. For the Connecticut Feminists in the Arts, I co-produced a musical review and designed a book of poetry. Before the Women's Movement and before Anais, I thought it was very unnatural to love women but since then I learned it is as natural as a bird's wing.

Anne McGovern: I'm a writer. Besides being intrigued by Nin and writing, I was intrigued by these two women who could get a group like this together.

May Garelick: I write books for children. When I was growing up everyoody I knew read Anais Nin. Now I find that all the young people I know are reading her books and are most enthusiastic. I'm here tonight for them too.

Evelyn Hinz speaks hurriedly, nervously: I'm a Canadian, so I'm an outsider here. I'm also a critic and that probably puts me in bad order. I want to talk tomorrow when I speak to you about Nin and her work, specifically how I came to her, so I'll just tell you now that I'm from Saskatchewan and it's very cold up there. About five years ago we had one of our worst winters but suddenly about mid-December there was a warm breeze which made everything unusually calm and beautiful in Saskatchewan. The weather officials and politicians were called in to find out where this warm breeze had come from. Finally someone recognized that there was a steady stream coming from the University Library. They traced it to the second floor. In fact in the American Literature section, in fact under N. **House of Incest.** And so Saskatchewan became very warm as a result of Nin's coming there. Seriously, I was introduced to Nin's work by a man, an uncouth-looking, bearded man, probably the kind of man you wouldn't expect to be interested in Nin's work but maybe that's an aspect that needs exploring.

David Williams: I try to make a film whenever I can. From what I hear one of the most likely ways to come across your writing is through a gift from a friend. And that's the first way I did. I skipped the Henry Miller stage. Henry Miller came after you. I think once you mentioned that the three most important things in your life were relationships, friendships and travel. I'm just beginning to grapple with those three things, and I would like to know more.

Jeffrey Mundy: I'm an artist and live in Washington, D.C. I first heard about Anais several years ago when a girlfriend of mine was reading her book for a year. I kept saying, 'Aren't you finished yet?' After I read it, I carried it around with *me* for a year. Through Anais I discovered that I must become a whole person and that in order to become the artist I wanted to be, I had to read and draw or paint and write.

Shirley McConahay: I used to be an historian. I taught and with my husband collaborated on a book called *Explorations in Sex and Violence.* We spent several summers at the Kinsey Institute for Sexual Research, and I came away very intrigued with personal sex relationships. Then through your books I became caught up in looking at the world through feelings, how we split ourselves up and then struggle to bring ourselves back together.

Nadine Daily: Legitimately, I'm an architect, but clandestinely, I'm an astrologer, poet and philosopher. I recently took eight months off to write a novel, because I was tired of building monuments to the living dead. I rented my apartment to a friend of mine while I went away. When I came back there was a gift to me - a volume of the *Diaries* - and a letter from her saying, 'I think you and Anais Nin have something in common. It's about time you met.' I didn't read the *Diary* then as I was too busy writing myself. About three weeks ago I went to the book store and spookily picked out *Novel of the Future* as the book I had to read. I read it and immediately after heard about Magic Circles and this weekend. I figured, that if I got the money from somewhere I would come. The money came, as it always has when something must be, so I called up Adele and said, "Okay, is there any room?" I got in just under the wire.

Ann Roche: I write for a newspaper and have done public relations work. I'm like a lot of women who started out very interested in writing and then something along the way happened to prevent it from happening. I became commercially oriented. When I was in college, there was a girl there who I always wanted to be: Sylvia Plath. When I heard that she had committed suicide, I felt that she had been punished by divine retribution for having achieved so much. My feeling was that a woman like her just can't make it. Then I met Valerie Sheehan and some of the other people in the Women's Liberation Movement and new doors opened. I started to believe again that women artists could make it and that's really why I'm so glad to be here.

Joan Anacreon: I'm a painter. A few years ago I narrowly escaped drowning, which turned out to be a fortunate experience because I really began to live after that incident. I began to say yes to living and to paint seriously.

Anais Nin rises from her chair at the front of the room and smiles. She is responding to us but her words seem to go out of the room to people everywhere.

Nadine: The heavy vibrations as we introduce ourselves. Each person as they speak creates an aura of themselves potently explosive for personalization at other moments.

Trew: I hear, 'Anais is my only friend! She is who I am inside. Through Nin I learned to be who I am.' With all these simple phrases, the beauty is not only in the words, but in the earnest and honest open quality with which they are spoken.

26

CHAPTER FOUR
ANAIS NIN: LIFE AS CELEBRATION

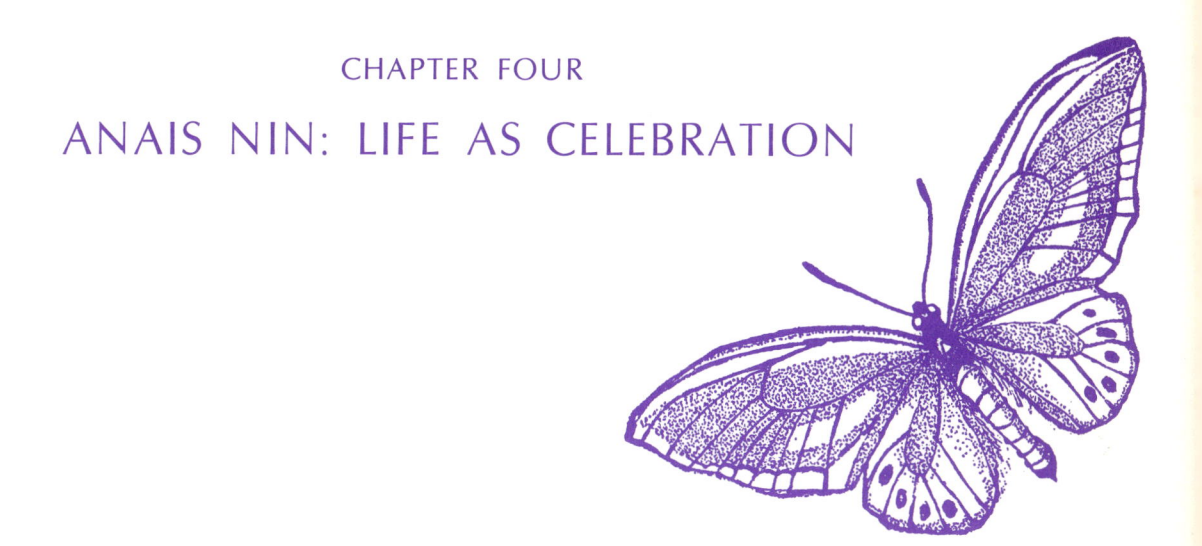

After all you have said, I became aware how closely knit we are. When you were making a portrait of your relation to my work, you were really revealing yourselves. I said, 'please introduce yourselves, please tell us about you.' It means that in speaking sometimes of my creations you are also speaking of **your** diaries, **your** creations, **your** paintings. My writing and your sculpture are all one thing. We need the source of it and the inspiration of it and all that is the same too. It's also taken from friendship and from love and from working together. I think that the isolated artist is always in greater danger of losing the very thing that he / she was creating because the whole purpose of creation was really mutual.

I had to answer the way you spoke about yourselves in relation to my work, how much I received of our oneness and your own personalities, but what I wanted was really to open the Weekend and explain the word 'celebration'. You proved to me what we do have to celebrate, all of us having an expression of some kind, an articulateness, a language, whether in painting or sculpture or in writing so that we could reveal this wonderful moment that is taking place, especially for women. I think women were the least articulate of artists. Their self-confidence was not very great. They were very dependent on those around them. And I think for the first time this is the moment when women are beginning to discover their identity. So we are celebrating this moment for women.

We are celebrating that we have heroes in an anti-hero culture. We have Ellsberg and Nader and women heroines. We have people who are willing to live in houseboats with very little money, like the artist Varda whose film you will see later. We have people dedicated to their work and the liberation of women. We have marvelous things to celebrate in a world that seems sometimes to cause despair.

To me, everyone who writes, everyone who articulates the position of woman or her feelings, everyone who creates anything, a house, a child, is an artist. It's not only in the art medium that we create. We create when we are working for someone or some cause, like the magazines that have been made with great effort and sometimes without much help. We are celebrating editors of magazines. We say we don't care, but we do. We are celebrating women like Beatrice Harris who are going forward in psychology. As a woman I think it is important at this moment to give woman an equal place. Someone was saying, give woman an equal place, let's eliminate man and woman and just say 'artists', but we are not ready yet. Museums don't say artists. They say, woman artist, and there are fewer women artists in museums than there are men. There is a need of equalization in the work. And we have heard about women who worked bringing the coffee when they should have been doing something else. I have had friends who were reporters like the beautiful intelligent woman, Jill Krementz, who made the photograph of me in the poster. Jill always wanted to be a real reporter. She was on duty one night at "Time Magazine" when the Harlem riots broke out and instead of calling for help she went there. Her boss said, 'Why didn't you call a man?' She said, 'Well, I was here and here are the photographs.' The man was in a state of shock. So we are celebrating here the strength of expression, the need of expression, the need of a language whatever this language is, whether it's film, words, paint. We are celebrating film makers here.

We are celebrating people who know how to live with very little money, as Varda did, making a beautiful life for himself. When he couldn't treat his friends to an enormous dinner, he made fried potatoes and red wine and that was it. (She laughs gaily) He did it so graciously that it seemed like a feast. We are celebrating Bebe Herring who went to Ireland and brought back a word called 'furrawn' which I stole and use in my lectures, because I love the significance of it. The kind of talk that leads strangers to intimacy — you can achieve this, and it doesn't matter if you're twenty or ten or one to one, provided you drop the persona, that terrible layer of false self which we adopt as a defense, and address the inner self, the vulnerable self. We also must take the risk of sharing.

Sharing the *Diary* was a risk. You may not believe that the dream I had was a nightmare but before publication I dreamed that I opened my front door and that I was struck by fatal radiation. That's how afraid I was. So you see, fear is there. The fear is in all of us and it is this fear we have to dispel. In friendship we realize that as human beings we are afraid to share, we are afraid to be criticized, we are afraid to be misunderstood, we are afraid not to be loved. This comes from childhood, from the teacher, from way back — I don't want to go as far back as we have to go to find out the origin of the fear. But women were very cowed with this fear. Their confidence was very much dependent on with whom they lived. I've seen women ask like children, 'Is this good?' They take their reflection in others. It is this confidence that the *Diary* may have given you because it does show the weak moments, it shows the anxieties, the retrogressions, how often I was blocked in my work or fearful, how often I depended on the opinion of others.

In the first *Diary* I was accused of narcissism because I used to write in a notebook everything nice that people used to say to me. It wasn't because I believed it: it was because I needed it to keep going. Critics misunderstood that. If I had thought those things of myself I wouldn't have written down what everybody was saying. I needed the opinion of others to grow. So it's in *Diary I* but gone from *Diary II*. But I think it shows a feminine lack of confidence, her pattern, who she is and her image. We are all working tremendously hard now to make distinctions, because I think there are feminine elements in men and there are masculine elements in women, and we have to achieve a chemical balance. Baudelaire said that in every one of us there is a man, a woman and a child, so we have to find in what proportion they are there and that makes the relationship to others very important.

We are celebrating everything that humans do to elevate themselves above the human condition. If we lived with only news and television and newspapers, we couldn't bear it. The whole structure is false. Now we know the hypocrisies, all the faults and false values with which we have been living, and we are occupied now in peeling these off, politically, historically, psychologically, humanly because they are making distance between us. Racial differences, origin, class, sex — are what we are trying to dispel. The most wonderful way is to communicate from core to core, from center to center. Our culture made an effort at finding the core of the self, but we put a taboo on it. It asserted that the self was selfish. I was very touched by the women who have done visibly useful things, such as speech therapy for 17 years or social work. I used to say, those people are really doing useful things, what am I doing? And then I suddenly realized that it was important to speak and simply articulate the struggle of our own evolution, because after all it is the only thing we really know. In noting all of the journey's steps, I was doing something useful, but I didn't know how much. What I was doing was fighting our battle.

So we have to celebrate this unity which makes us very interdependent and necessary to each other. Let us say that from this certain moment we have this degree of strength, this degree of vision, this courage, but there are times we lack all of them and then someone else has to give it to us. Let's celebrate what we bring to each other, what we share with each other, how much of the persona we can peel off. I notice two of you are artists in masks; the masks we have worn have always frightened people. I used to dress to frighten away my enemies. All this is useful and adolescent but it's very significant to what we feel when unmasked and sharing feelings. Strangely enough, the radiation I dreamed of at the front door never took place. What took place was great intimacy and sense of interdependence.

In another room we watch Agnes Varda's film about her late uncle, the famous artist, Jean Varda. It is called "Uncle Yanko" and is an ebullient narrative-collage of his life-style and work.

Afterwards, people talk or write in their private journals until late at night, tending to the circus going on in their heads.

Nadine: I don't even remember what I said, the movie and much chatter came with cumulative effect to a crescendo. I watched the aura of each group, stood as in the eye of a hurricane the calm before the storm of new adventure, watching bits and pieces of my psyche scattered reconnaissance then quiet distillation to the quiet of my treefilled window.

Adele: I feel layers of defenses shed and drop to the ground. I am becoming transparent!

Joan: At this point the conventional structure of time fell away for me. I said to Sas, 'This is like I died and went to Heaven. If there really is a Heaven I would like it to be like this, with people being real to each other!'

Trew: (It is) Saturday morning and my system responds to these new energies. I awake by 5:30 a.m., the sun already touching the nylon mist of the small bedroom window. I go outside watching the gulls and ducks flop about on the surface of the water with plaintive cries. Across the Sound is a constant roar of motor nose, like the take-off of a jet plane which never takes off. It is New York traffic. Living here one must grow to integrate such things but I find the big city a monster I do not understand.

32

CHAPTER FIVE

FRANCES STELOFF REMINISCES

"I never said no to anything"

As we gather to listen to Frances, the mood is intense and serious. People are still borne by the tide of deep conversations held during the night. It is slightly amazing to share breakfast and start a new day together.

In 1920 Frances Steloff founded the Gotham Book Mart on 47th Street in New York City. The Gotham is a literary institution, devoid of commercialism, well loved for its atmosphere of heroic disorder, having everything rare or modern, out-of-print treasures, a vast collection of theatre and film volumes, and 50,000 vintage "little" magazines.

Frances sits before us, wearing a yellow print dress and lavender shawl and shoes. In her hands she holds a family of dandelions — "Mother, father, and baby", she says. I am reminded of her affection for cats, how she allows her Putsy to cuddle on her chest at night, purring and licking her face, because she feels that she was starved for affection as a child. And how she makes sure at twilight that she does not miss seeing the sun set. She is so spiritual in her love of life and opposition to violence. Her wisdom seems simple and direct, but got with difficult concentration and discipline.

Anais Nin introduces Frances. This remarkable woman is a great inspiration to other women. In 1920 she opened up a bookshop near the theatre section of town. She had the idea of keeping the bookshop open in the evening for people who came from the theatre. The shop was devoted to the dance and the theatre crowd mostly. But after that what she did was to create a bookshop which was far more than a bookshop. Her own frustrated, unfulfilled love of books made her feel that she wanted to be surrounded by books. This was the seed and the origin of the bookshop. There she had her books all around her.

She had this extraordinary hospitality, so people began to make of her bookshop a center, a center for the Joyce Society, a center where many people met each other, and many literary friendships were made. It was the warmth and hospitality which gave the bookshop its character. By her saying yes to everything, like Caresse Crosby, 'yes' to magazines and 'yes' to unknown writers and 'yes' to unknown books, she created a treasury in the cellar. The books you couldn't find anywhere else, you found in the Gotham Book Mart.

Her achievement as a woman, keeping this warm place not only as a bookshop but as a center for friendship and relationships to writers and critics and poets, makes tremendous literary history, which has not been written as fully and richly as it should have been. She was too modest to do it herself. Frances Steloff couldn't possibly tell you all the things she could.

Frances Steloff: *(Frances delights in telling humorous stories about herself that break everyone up into raucous laughter. At the same time she projects the seriousness and inner light of a Pilgrim.)*

I think the Gotham Book Mart just grew because of people like Anais. She will never know what it meant in those early days to have a letter from her saying that the Book Mart is well known to us on the Left Bank and for her to have the confidence to send all her books and tell me to use my own judgment about price. But there are many wonderful people who had this confidence. I seem to have been a natural born catalyst. I just had this very strong urge to get the right books, special books, into the people's hands. I often judged my books by the people who bought them.

When salesmen brought certain books, I'd say, 'Oh, this one is good', and they'd look at me wonderingly because I'd order very large quantities for a small shop. I'd say, 'This is important, everybody ought to have this.' I thought all I would have to do is have the book here and everybody would realize what a wonderful book it was. I would put it in the window, get cards printed, and put it in our catalogue. In this way I didn't know that I was doing this for others but just because I felt that it had to be done.

I didn't take books because of large discounts! In one instance I felt a book on hypnotism wasn't right, because it is wrong to take control of other people's minds. When the salesman said, 'This book is a best seller,' I said, 'I can't sell books on hypnotism.' Then the author came in and wanted to know what I had against his book. I said that I just don't believe that it's right to encourage people to become passive and let other people control your mind. I think he understood finally but it took a lot of explaining.

I had the same feeling for people. For instance, the Joyce Society was born because Professor Tindall at Columbia had James Joyce Seminars, and sent his students to the Gotham for books by and about Joyce. The students were always asking questions that I couldn't answer so I thought somebody ought to have a study group on Joyce. I asked two or three of my customers — John Slocum was one, because he had a wonderful collection of Joyce — to lead a group of Joyce students.

Oh no, Slocum couldn't be bothered. I asked James Gilvarry — a Dubliner who has a great collection of Irish authors — he said, no, but he'd give me his private telephone number if I needed to ask questions. I saw Roland von Weber, who was acting in Joyce's **Exiles**. I went backstage and asked him after the play but being an actor meant he couldn't always be around. So I thought, well I'll just have to wait until I find somebody.

One day, one of my nice customers who was a lawyer, a very fatherly sort of person, said, 'How are things and what are your problems?'

'I've always had problems', I said chuckling, 'Well you know, there ought to be a study group for Joyce because all these young ones come in and ask questions and we ought to find answers for them.'

He said, 'Well do you know anybody?'

'Yes, I've asked them but they're not willing to take it on.'

He said, 'Give me their names and telephone numbers.' And I did. In a week he called up and asked, 'Would it be all right to come over this evening?'

'Why yes of course.'

So he came along with a set of people, like Ted McKnight Kauffer, the publisher, McNight Alpert, the artist, and a lot of wonderful people, who knew Joyce but whom I wouldn't think of approaching. We talked about it. I said that I'd be happy to have them meet here but I couldn't do any more. Then I worked up front and let them have their own way of deciding.

When they left, they said, 'We'll be back. In a few days they called up: 'This is the 3rd of February 1947 — the day after Joyce's birthday — can we come tonight?'

'Yes, of course.'

That was the night that the Joyce Society was born. And everything else happened in the same way. The thing seemed to take form. The people that were meant to do these things came and did them. I really had very little to do with it.

Anais: That's what you say, but Professor Tindall says in a letter that you were the Joyce Society.

Frances: He's just being generous.

Anais: Tell us the story of how you made the window of women's work?

Frances: When Anais finally came in person to the Gotham I was grateful and showed it. Anais talked to me about not being able to find a publisher and her courage to go out and buy a press. What an undertaking it was to find a press and then to learn to run it and set type! This was no small accomplishment. She did it beautifully but of course she is a perfectionist. At the time the Book Mart had a huge window. I thought it would be great to have a window on the theme "Women At Work." I tried to get one of those signs, 'Men At Work', and all the people I asked thought I was a bit goofy. Finally I had to have a sign made called "Women At Work". I collected all the books by women for the window display.

Anais: This was in the 40's wasn't it? The beginning of Feminism!

Frances: Yes, also I had a picture of Anais working at her press, showing the making of a book from the beginning of the manuscript to the end.

Well, that's how things happened at the shop. Everything came. I didn't reach out really. I always said 'yes' to everyone who came to the shop. I thought that if they came to me this was an opportunity for me to be helpful; at the same time I was helping myself.

In all my most wonderful experiences people came with a problem, something they needed, and I helped them. I believe that first you learn to give and then you get. Usually people say, 'How many hours do I have to work?' and 'how much do you pay?' but they never think what do I have to give or am I qualified? That's true today more than ever and I think this attitude is one of the reasons for the condition we're in.

Now, what else can I tell you?

Daisy Aldan: I would like to say that in 1946 when I was a young teacher and poet and made a book with wallpaper and laundry cardboards and calligraphy, I wanted to take it to the Gotham Book Mart first of all. The same boy who had first given me Anais' book helped me take it there. He went in and I waited outside trembling, sure that Miss Steloff would never take it. I knew how the Gotham was the place where everybody knew you could get Anais' books and all the books of poetry and I badly wanted my book there.

When the boy came out, he said, 'She's some character! I was afraid to talk to her, but she took your book! I was very thrilled about that. But she didn't put them out for sale. She was saving them for something! A few years ago when the Gotham Book Mart gave a party for me, I saw one of those books for sale at such a tremendous price that I couldn't buy it. But Frances probably never realized what encouragement she was to me. Later on she gave my magazine, **Folder Editions**, *a window display.*

Frances: I tried to display every magazine and book that came in. So many of the authors would expect to see their work in the window whenever they came by. In fact they made special trips to check on it, but others had to have a chance too. Some of the young magazine editors, the real youngsters, didn't have the money to even buy the materials to make a magazine.

I'd say, 'can't you find a magazine to publish your poems without starting another one?'

'No, No!' No magazine was just right for their poems. Either the table of contents had to be in the back or it had to be in the middle . . . ! They felt that if I would put their magazine in the window they'd be assured of success. I always did, I never failed them.

The same way with the parties. People thought that if the Gotham would give them a party, that's it! There was an author in Boston, published by Harvard University, who asked if we'd have a party in our garden.

I asked, 'Are you all coming from Boston?'

The publishers said that they allot a certain amount of money for publicity for everything they publish and that the author said he would rather have a party at the Gotham than any other publicity. So they all came. The garden was wonderful because parties didn't take any preparation. When we moved to where we are now, we no longer had the garden but had the back room, which gave us the advantage of having parties year round. But it was a lot of work to empty it each time. We put everything on wheels, or made it collapsible, like a stage set. We'd have to take all the books off the tables and set up a big board. I don't think I ever refused a party for a book, so a great many people were encouraged, the young ones especially. I saw so many young people go wrong in the pool rooms and race tracks of Saratoga Springs that when I saw a young one do something useful and interesting like writing, I was eager to help. I never turned a deaf ear to a young person!

Valerie: Frances, you were a very courageous young person, being on your own in New York at the age of 17.

Frances: Everything in my early life seems to have been a preparation for what was to come. When I was living in Boston my older sister was getting married, and there was a family reunion in New York. My aunt said to me, 'Well, why go back to Boston if your sister is being married. Stay with me in Brooklyn.'

That was okay with me so I went to work at Loeser's Department Store in the corset department. I was grateful to be anywhere in those days. A job was very difficult to find and I thought this would satisfy me temporarily.

Christmas came and the floorwalker said that I was to work at a temporary book table. Well, I was delighted to be with books instead of corsets. Every evening at 6:00, closing time, a man would come to replace the books that had been sold. I never hurried away like the other girls did.

One night he said, 'If you like the books so much why don't you ask the buyer to keep you here?'

'Who is the buyer?'

He told me and the next day I watched for him but he looked very discouraging! I thought, I can't talk to him today, but maybe tomorrow. I walked trembling up to him and asked if I might stay in the book department instead of going back to corsets. 'Ho, Ho,' he said. 'We have all we can do to keep our own staff and we can't make room for any new people.'

I thought, 'Oh dear, my last hope gone.'

I reluctantly turned away and then he said, 'Wait a minute, wait a minute, do you know anything about magazines?'

'No, but I can learn very quickly.'

And he took me over to where the carriage trade was, near the swinging doors. He said, 'This girl is always out sick.' I said, 'Oh, I'm *never* sick.' There was nothing between this long counter and the outdoors but swinging doors. There was a constant draft! I thought that I would just wear plenty of clothes. I wore two pairs of stockings and all the sweaters I could find. So that's how I started in the book business.

A man there in the old rare books department would often come over and ask how was I doing. I'd always say fine. After about a year he asked if I'd gotten a raise.

I said, 'no.' He said that I should go up to Mr. Cooper and tell him how I had doubled the business in the department. So finally after much urging I went up. I was afraid of Mr. Cooper too — he had bulging eyes. But I promised that I would go up and I did.

I told him that we were selling so much more. He said, 'the more you sell, the more we lose.' I didn't know how to figure that one, but I learned it was because Loeser's and Abraham & Straus were always competing, and if one sold more books, the other would lower the prices, so in the end, the more I sold, the more they lost. 'I can't give you a raise.'

I was getting $7.00 a week. My friend was annoyed and said that he would get me a job at Schulte's.

I rather dreaded to make a change because I loved my magazines. However, I never could say no to anything and so I landed at Schulte's, a real bookstore. I had charge of the circulating library and the Sunday School supplies.

One day, Ms. McDevitt-Wilson, who had a beautiful book shop, came in to look for some out-of-print books and I was able to help her. She was pleased and whispered to me as she was going out and said, 'If you ever consider making a change come and see me.'

McDevitt Wilson's meant one less streetcar fare for me, so I went down to see her. She offered me $8.00, a raise of $1.00. I was very happy there for three years.

Cora McDevitt loved poetry. She was very spontaneous and if there weren't any customers around, she'd say, 'Girls, do you know this by Kipling?' Then she'd recite his poetry. In those days Kipling was a modern like Dylan Thomas. I loved it. One time she recited "The Painted Desert", which is about the joy of working. No one shall work for money, but for the joy of working. This struck home.

Eventually I left there. One of the girls wanted me to go to Maine for our vacation. I made arrangements but in the meantime one of the mail order boys left and Mr. Wilson asked me not to go.

I said, 'It's the end of the summer and nobody takes vacations after Labor Day.' He said, 'Well if you want to go, you needn't come back.'

This was a great blow, but I went to Maine. I thought I'd never have such an opportunity. The place I was to go cost only $5.00 a week and had animals — a newborn calf, dogs and cats — all the animals that I love, so I went.

I never went back to McDevitt-Wilson's, but after my vacation I went to Brentano's, my last job before starting the Gotham Book Mart.

One day I was going over to the Astor Hotel to see my sister who was working there in the office, and as I was crossing 45th Street, I saw this homemade sign in a window. It said, 'space for rent.' This was in December 1919. In those days space was very rare, because during the War there had been no building. The milliners and dress shops were merging with jewelry shops. I went over to the door and could see sewing machines and girls at work. I went in to see it and was thrilled at the thought of having a room for nothing but books. My spine began to burn, and I thought, 'This is it! THIS IS IT!'

The rent was $75.00 a month, and I asked for an option until the next day. I had liberty bonds that I could cash and had collected some out-of-print books on the theatre. A friend told me that it was good for a book shop to be on the downtown side of the street. He said also not to worry about what books to stock, but to let my customers educate me. He thought I just might make a go of it, which was the most encouraging thing anyone had said. And finally he advised that if I did take the shop to make sure my first customer was a young person.

I paid my first month's rent and then looked around for a carpenter to build shelves. I had one bookcase, a desk, a table and chair. New Year's Day my friends found a horse and wagon and loaded it with my books and helped me to get settled as well as they could. I didn't have enough books to fill even one side of the wall. So I stretched out the books, spreading them all out as wide as I could. The first day I saw an old man tottering down the stairs holding on to the bannister. I didn't know whether to be thankful or not, as we didn't have the book he wanted. The next day I saw a handsome young man looking in the window. I had one book on costumes. I opened it as wide as I could on the floor of this little window. I said to myself, 'if only he would come in and find a book!'

I no sooner had the thought when down the steps came this young man who said, 'Can I see that book — that costume book?' Boy, I went to the window and laid it out on the table. It was the most expensive book I had — $15.00

He took out $10.00 and said, 'Here's the deposit. After the matinee I will pick it up.' He gave me a little card, which said Mr. Glenn Hunter.

I thought, 'Oh, my first sale and an actor!' 'And handsome and young!' As he went out, I saw him duck into the stage entrance near by the theatre where Billie Burke and Glenn Hunter were in Booth Tarkington's play, *Seventeen*. Again I said, 'Oh my first sale!' I couldn't afford to frame the $10.00 bill. If it had been $1.00, I would have kept it.

That started me off. I asked Glenn afterwards when we became very dear friends, why he came back after every matinee and very often in the evening on the way to a performance?

He said, 'I came back because I felt there was a *need*.'

A NEED — that stayed in my mind. Of course by the time that I asked him, I was in the next shop, where we had more books than we had room for. Everytime he came it was wonderful. He told all his friends, like Helen Hayes and Billie Burke.

Across the street from the shop a play, *The Gold Diggers,* with Ina Claire was the hit of Broadway. All of the cast would come over and that's how I came to stay open until midnight. I just felt that I couldn't disappoint anybody. So I was there. Then Ina Claire decided that she eeded a vacation, and David Belasco said that if she insisted on having a vacation the play would have to close. And it did, which was a great loss to me.

I had a hard time getting through the summer after *The Gold Diggers* left. By that time I had opened an account with Baker and Taylor's who carried books of all publishers. I shocked their proper old salesman once when I ordered 500 copies of J.M. Barries' one act plays. I would always get uncontrollably excited about some books! It was pure honest enthusiasm that made me order 500 copies, but Mr. Scribner, the publisher, was so impressed that he wrote a whole page in appreciation of my interest in their one act plays. And after that Scribner's let me take books on consignment. Things like that were always happening to me. In those days we didn't have books on consignment. If a book didn't sell we were stuck with it. But he said that I could have these on consignment and not pay for them until they sold. If I needed an extension of time, he'd arrange it. I never knew there could be such kindness.

So I got beautiful art books on my shelves. I thought I would have to be in business for years before I could stock books like that. But this is how we build Karma. This enabled the book shop to go on.

At another point I had so many expenses that I thought it was goodbye, little shop, goodbye. I saw a man looking in the window one day. He didn't look as if he could buy any books. He wore baggy pants and a soft shirt. His hair was tousled. He didn't look at all important. But he came down and began to look at the books on the tables. Then he stacked them on the chair.

I thought, 'What's he doing that for?' He kept picking up these books and after awhile he didn't even look in the books, he just looked at the covers and put them on the chair.

When the books were piled up to the top of the back of the chair, he said, 'Can you get those around to me at the Hippodrome?'

I said, 'Yes, of course.' I never said no to anything. I asked a boy to take the books for me. I counted up the books — almost all my stock — and the bill came to $299.00. Then I realized what a fool I'd been because the boy might never collect the money and I didn't even know the buyer's name. Well, I was terribly worried, thinking about all the money I owed for the books, and how the Gotham Book Mart was ruined forever.

And then the boy came back smiling and holding a great big roll of singles! I began to dance around the table! I said 'I can pay my rent, and I can pay my gas, and I can pay all my bills and have money left over.' That was a pretty close call, but I came through. This man R. H. Burnside was the greatest of the Hollywood directors now at the Hippodrome. I asked him afterwards when we became friends, how he happened to come in and he gave the same answer that Glenn did, that he felt there was a need and he could use the books.

There were a lot of close calls the Gotham had before it finally got on its feet. But something always happened to rescue it, often at the last minute when I thought there was no hope. Yet, I always seemed to know it. It happened so many times that I thought it's not me that's running the shop but it's in keeping with the *Plan*. . . (She is given a long vigorous applause).

Valerie: You certainly survived doing what you wanted to do.

Frances: Very often I'm asked if such a venture could succeed today. I say, 'yes if you have the ingredients.'

Kitty: What are the ingredients?

Frances: The ingredients are a capacity for self-denial, and hard work. Not work that you consider drudgery, for there is no such thing as drudgery unless you make it that. You must love your work and look upon it as an opportunity. **When you are doing a job out in the world you are at the same time doing a job inside yourself.** And you must have the capacity and the integrity to do it. It never was difficult for me to go down to work before 9:00. I shoveled the snow and swept the sidewalk and I did whatever there was to be done. Nothing was menial. I did it lovingly.

I had a boy, a shipping clerk, and told him that he was to sweep. He said that he didn't go four years to high school to come here and sweep. I thought, 'Well, you are not the right one for me then.' That's when I became firm — I was supposed to be a very hard hearted person whom people feared — but if a person can't do the things that need to be done, then he doesn't belong there.

(Turning to Anais)

Now that's where I take issue with my darling here. You take on everybody's problems. You let them lean on you until you can hardly stand up on your own feet. I'm sorry, but I have to disagree with that. I think you are not doing them a favor when you take on their responsibilities. I think it is law that we help people bear their responsibility but not take it away from them. It reminds me of what Krishna says about it being better to do your own work imperfectly than to do another person's work well.

I had all the work I could do to survive. This was my responsibility. I would put everybody's books in the window. I would catalogue them and tell people about them. I loved books even without reading them, I felt instinctively when books offered something. Of course I had members of my family that I had to help. But I would help them as much as I could without jeopardizing that for which I was responsible. I think it's better to let people carry their own responsibility. It makes them stronger. It gives them the experience that they need. After a certain point you are interfering with their Karma, by taking them on so completely. My heart ached when you were helping all these people to the point where you were actually ill.

Anais: But that was only a stage. A phase.

Frances: But you could deplete yourself so that you couldn't go on with your own work.

Anais: But I was convinced that writers needed help.

Frances: Oh, how I used to quarrel with Henry Miller about that! He thought that they should be financially supported and I thought that they should not. They should be given a chance, could borrow money while they needed it, without interest, on a time limit, but they must understand that they have to pay it back. He disagreed and threatened never to come into the shop again. But I didn't realize all that you had gone through until I read the fourth Volume of your *Diary*. I wish I had kept up writing my Journal.

Anais: It is a pity that Rogers in his book about the Gotham, *Wise Men Fish Here*, couldn't write a better book about you.

Frances: I was very unhappy about that book. When he asked to do it, I thought he was a good choice, because he had written a book about Gertrude Stein, one of the "moderns". I thought he was "with" us. He used my manuscript, but he didn't have the feeling for it. He didn't seem to be interested in the things I thought were important. Eventually I lost all interest in it but allowed it to be published. To my great surprise it got very good reviews. Marianne Moore told me she read it again and again because she found encouragement in it for herself.

Anais: All the facts were there. It was the story of overcoming great obstacles, but it wasn't inspiring. He told it too plain and simple. You tell the story much better in your own words.

In the end Frances does not want to accept her lecturer's fee but to give it to Anais, to us, or the staff at Wainwright House, least of all to herself. She felt rewarded enough by everyone's response to her, yet it was she who had given herself as a gift first. In the same way she sold the books of writers and artists and through the love and art of serving them she was rewarded by distinction and honor of her own.

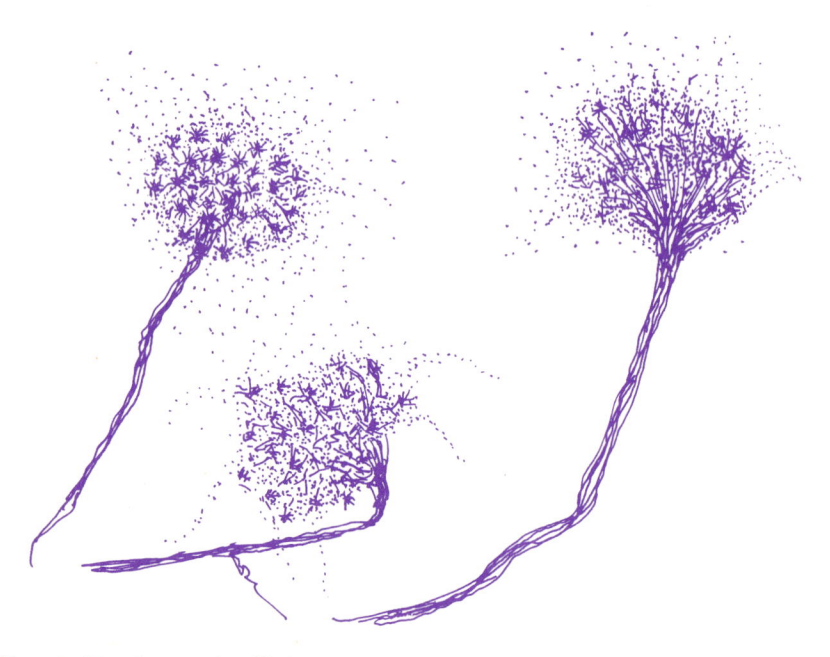

Joan: The tears well up inside of me and spill down my cheeks in an unending flow. Her story is one of absolute faith in spite of overwhelming obstacles. Frances is a person who has given birth to her dream. Such a person is rare and precious . . . Here at this weekend the magic was that I was surrounded by people who were not afraid to dream and make the dreams tangible realities.

Nadine: Feeling the determination of Frances, the synchronicity. If you're doing what is right for you to do, it will happen, out of the respect for oneself that comes from working at something you love.

Adele: Frances at eight-four still in flow and growing, asking "What next?" She comes up to me and says, "When you asked me to come here I didn't think I belonged. Now I see why you asked me, how I fit in, how I lived my life the way it was intended." A true innocent. I could not believe she was who she is and not really feel the importance of her role in the lives of creators. Suppose she had missed that awareness! I realized how little people say to each other when they have achieved something. The world assumes Frances Steloff does not need to be told but that is not true.

45

46

CHAPTER SIX

WILLIAM CLAIRE:

THE RELEVANCE OF LITERARY MAGAZINES

William Claire is the founding editor and publisher of "Voyages", a national literary magazine, of which Anais Nin has been a contributor and advisor. His poems have appeared in "The Antioch Review", "Nation", "American Scholar", "New Republic", "New York Quarterly", and elsewhere. He appears contained and proper in a dark blue suit. His voice is deep and friendly.

Anais introduces him: I first met Bill Claire through "Voyages". The title appealed to me very much and I was pleased to be put on the advisory board. The magazine always had beautiful photographs and articles about the poets. Bill Claire, himself, would send you poems occasionally on yellow paper while he was attending interminable meetings, as a lobbyist for peace. He was a poet too and very modest about it. (To Claire) I don't think you published your own things in your magazine?

WILLIAM CLAIRE: Nothing.

ANAIS: That's being over-modest.

WILLIAM CLAIRE: I'm delighted to be here but Miss Steloff is a very tough act to follow. I hope everybody has been to The Gotham. I've been a book nut all of my life and have been in every used book store in the United States and some abroad, and consider The Gotham Book Mart certainly the best in the country - and for literary magazine people, it's everything.

Frances: I've seen you there.

WILLIAM: "Voyages" for six years has always sold out at The Gotham Book Mart, which is not true in any other store so it's wonderful to share the morning with you.

Anais was of great value to my magazine as an advisory editor from the beginning. She was not at all like another famous man whom I wrote to of my dreams for starting a magazine and his being an advisory editor. I said there had never been anything like this in Washington where I live. He wrote back and said he'd be delighted to be an advisory editor if I took his advice. I wrote back and said sure, "What's your advice?"

He said, "Don't start a literary magazine." But he did become an advisory editor and a very good one. But the importance of Anais was that through her I was put in touch with several writers whom I published: Marguerite Young - on whom I hope to do a special issue some day, because she is one of the most compelling writers of our time; - Daisy Aldan, E.M. Esker on the West Coast, poet Natalie Robbins from New York, Wayne McEvilly in Mexico, and several others who have given a certain flavor to the magazine.

(To Anais) I'm deeply grateful to you for that. You kept me in touch with writers all over the world. Some I haven't published. I never had the feeling that if you sent me a piece there was any compulsion to publish it and so some were sent back. But unlike any other advisory editor you have contributed to the flavor of the magazine, for which I am deeply grateful.

Now about the possible importance of literary magazines in our society - in early days I published in much the same way Thomas Merton, the Trappist monk, described in connection with some drawings that he published in magazines:

In a world cluttered and programmed with an infinity of practical signs and consequential digits referring to business, law, government, and war, one who makes such non-descript marks as these is conscious of a special vocation to be inconsequent, to be outside the sequence, and to remain firmly alien to the program. In effect these writings are decidedly hopeful in their own way insofar as they stand outside all processes of production, marketing, consumption and destruction, which does not mean however that they cannot be bought. Nevertheless it is clear that these are not legal marks nor are they illegal marks since as far as law is concerned they are perfectly inconsequent. And to be perfectly inconsequent in terms of the supposed consequential matters is to me the essence of a literary magazine. This presumes that the more advanced a technological society becomes, the more important individual endeavors are, in a practical sense. Not only for the purpose of one's sanity but also because it is the only way civiluzation, if it deserves to advance at all, might proceed.

At another level, Primus St. John, a black poet friend of mine from the inner-city, once wrote me, **'WHEN THE WORLD GETS YOU DOWN, FOOL IT WITH A POEM.'** The same point of view applies to all your endeavors from pottery to painting.

Unfortunately, little magazines have to deal with outside influences like distributors, post offices, whose increasing rates threaten to drive many of them out of business, and others who would like to exploit the magazine for one purpose or another. Even in a private endeavor with a total sense of independence, you have to deal with those who would want in some way to subvert it or to have you sell out. And there is nothing that disturbs the Establishment more than something they cannot understand and there's no conceivable way for them to understand a little magazine.

In reaction to this, however, some editors tend to become overly political. They become anarchists and act as if they are always marching against the Czar. And it's very difficult to march against the Czar with a mimeograph machine. You just can't win. So if I ever have another magazine and publish a manifesto I will probably have a blank page. I think it's good to rant and rave against the established forces, but I'm increasingly inclined to think that it would be just better to fill the world with poems, with stories, with photographs and make that kind of presence without preaching and I dare say often without politics. Although a magazine needs to resist even the pressures to resist, the best ones seem to move beyond the reflections of an individual's tastes and whatever limitations that might entail.

In the five or six years since I've had the good ship "Voyages" going, we've had many interesting trips. But I come here this weekend hoping to find from all of you possible new areas in which I may move, new areas that I would like to explore. Just as Wallace Stevens had a poem about "Thirteen Ways of Looking at a Blackbird", so I have developed 10 commandments for a literary magazine: These are not the 'shalt nots" of childhood repression, but 10 commandments for this gathering this weekend. Here they are:

1. Thou shalt try to discover new writers who are saying new things, or old things in new ways.

2. Thou shalt try to discover experienced writers who are saying old or new things in a way that is unique.

3. Thou shalt try to get experienced or old writers to say things that they didn't know they were capable of saying.

4. Thou shalt keep the magazine open to experimentation and styles of writing that you might not necessarily agree with.

5. Thou shalt provide writers with space in which to move about. Poems are not fillers in a magazine and deserve a full page.

6. Make each issue a new event and have each issue evolve in the process of development... For my own protection I should mention that several years ago I did an issue devoted to women writers.

7. Thou shalt attempt to produce a magazine that has good paper, printing, and design, which hopefully people will want to keep, not throw away like "The New York Times" or "Atlantic Monthly".

8. Thou shalt try to remain totally outside the commercial realm if possible and even the academic one, with all due apologies.

9. Also be wary of people with subsidies because my early experience was that the larger the subsidy, the more poems this person had to be published in a closet or drawer.

10. And, finally, thou shalt remember in the end that society will probably never admit that there is a price for this kind of magazine since it follows no prescribed rules, fits into no easy compartment, never, I hope, comes out on a regular basis; and the magazine to the best of its ability affirms continuing openness to new methods of expression and independence from any form of regimentation and generally tries to preserve its real virtue - humor - and the opportunity for hope that new writers can say whatever it is they have to say.

That is all I really want to say, but in connection with the question of treating the woman writer as woman rather than just as poet or artist, I'd like to add that recently I was talking with Gloria Steinem about her magazine, "Ms", and told her that I thought that she was missing most of the good writing that was going on in America by women, if not all. I mentioned unfamiliar names to her and simply said, "try to find these." I fear that possibly the women's thing may become exploitable by people who have the profit motive. When I did the woman's issue, I wrote the following note:

> *In a country as startlingly surrealistic as the United States, it is rarely a good idea to try to develop themes in anything at all. When that subject might happen to be woman, the whole notion of a unifying concept becomes absurd. This issue of "Voyages" started out to be a woman issue, but the notion was abandoned. No overview or underview of any kind is intended here although it will soon be obvious that most of the contributions happen to be by or about women. We are honored to call special attention to the American poet, Josephine Miles of California and Jane Cooper of New York City. Ms. Miles is the kind of well known poet about whom enough good things can never be said and Ms. Cooper is just on the verge of establishing herself through the publication of her first book due in 1969.*

This is the real sense of satisfaction: we did a special feature on Jane Cooper and six months later she won the Lamont Poetry Prize for her first book. So that's the real joy in literary magazines. It's nice to have the established writers and the famous writers but to... now I did not discover her... give writers like her special treatment before her first book, is something I like to remember. Then I had a long piece by Carolyn Gordon and Harry Peebles on Twiggy, of all people to show how outdated this is, although this article isn't dated. I was also extremely proud to publish the section by Anais on the relationship of her work to her famous **Diaries.** As I wrote:

> *If anybody could symbolize all of the finest qualities of the feminine gender, Anais Nin is that person. Her extraordinary role in literature is just beginning to be felt, although she has been in fact an international hero to writers and artists since the 1930's. There are too many other fine writers in this issue to single out by name but we hope the careful reader will note the divergence of styles, the various geographical background, and both the strangeness and sometimes startling clarity of some of the material. If it all seems too diverse, too strange, and ultimately lacking in any theme, so often goes the journey of the mind.*

This was my effort some five years ago of bringing together various women writers. I'm just trying to say I'm all for you.

Larry: Could you tell us quickly how you would start a magazine again, not necessarily in Washington, but in a similar city?

WILLIAM: You have to have the usual mixture of idealism and insanity, to confront all the problems. I was lucky because I knew the kinds of things I had to do. The wonderful quality about starting a literary magazine is that you don't know anything and you make 100 mistakes along the way. Everybody who has been in the business, rather non-business, since we've never been **in** business, will tell you not to go ahead. The problems are insurmountable. But the wonder of this in America and other countries is that no matter what you tell people, some will still go ahead. And I think that's a very healthy sign.

Valerie: Are you financially solvent?

WILLIAM: No.

Valerie: You don't think it's possible to have a self-sustaining literary magazine?

WILLIAM: I don't think so. Even the subsidized ones like "Kenyon Review" and others are slowly going out of existence. It's just impossible. It costs more to print an issue than you could ever sell it for.

Valerie: I read that there was one distributor named DeBoer for literary magazines in Hoboken, New Jersey and that because he was ill, a whole lot of literary magazines would never get to the market.

WILLIAM: That's probably true. Yes, although many magazine editors do not like to let distributors get their magazine, they make an awful lot of money on it, 50% or so. In my case I wanted the magazines back that did not sell. One distributor on the West Coast rips off the covers of the unsold ones. They take 50% or 60% before they start to sell and give you back damaged copies.

Ann Roche: Why do they rip off the covers?

WILLIAM: That's a distributor's method of showing how many copies didn't sell. Instead of sending the whole issue back they just send the cover to show they didn't sell it. It's okay to do to "Life," but to a magazine, "Voyages," it's a valuable loss.

Nancy Williamson: The distributor in Boston does the same thing with ''The Second Wave,'' the magazine we've been publishing in Boston. We thought that if we could only get a distributor, the magazine would be all over the U.S. on the book stands. But our distributor didn't tell us anything, except the percentage he would get. He didn't say that all he does is dump a package at the newsstand, where the owner of the stand then decides whether to put it on the stand or not. And our woman's movement magazine is clearly something that most men who run a newsstand do not want to sell. We would go around and find the magazines way in back with the pornographic stuff. We'd go in and talk to them and discover that if you offer the man at the newsstand 10% more than you're already giving the distributor, he'll put it out on the front shelf for maybe a few weeks. The magazine cost us 35¢ to print and sold for 75¢ with the distributor and newsstand men taking the difference. In the end we received very little money back but a lot of magazines with ripped off covers.

Valerie: Do you think that there is more activity in small magazines on the East Coast or the West Coast?

WILLIAM: In big population centers there are very few really first rate little magazine bookstores. San Francisco has some. The Gotham in New York, of course, is the greatest. The peculiar thing I found about my magazine is that interest came from incredible places like Bowsmith, Montana. But more people will buy copies in New York than in Washington. I don't have a distributor for "Voyages". I distribute them myself, putting some here, some there. The last subscription I received came from The Institute of Oceanography in Brazil. They think "Voyages" means sailing trips!

ANAIS: I think what lies behind the literary magazine or Magic Circles, is a wish to unify a circle of friends. It has never been a commercial thing. Many magazines are being collected now by universities as collector's items, because very famous writers were therein published before they were known. The whole history of the literary magazine is very beautiful and uncommercial. The magazines have been a great boon to the writers. So whenever I have a good writer that I know I can persuade, you know, to establish himself, I send him or her to you.

WILLIAM: The literary magazine has really been the best outlet for authors from Ezra Pound to you here.

*Daisy Aldan: For people like T.S. Eliot, Dylan Thomas, Ezra Pound, Caresse Crosby, before her **Portfolio** and Black Sun Press, and innumerable people who never gained public recognition, the little magazines always served their purpose. They contained the seeds that bear the future fruit.*

Valerie: How do you publicize "Voyages"?

WILLIAM: By word of mouth. It's just impossible to advertise. The cost of a little advertisement in something like "The New York Review of Books" is too much. Even in the "Washington Post", an ad costs something like $200. Full pages are $4,000. "The New Yorker" charges $25,000 for a half page.

Nancy Williamson: Do you exchange ads with other magazines?

WILLIAM: That's always a good thing to do.

Frances Steloff: I always felt that the publishers should contribute to the support of little magazines because they eventually get the benefit of them. They watch how an author develops with magazines. I think this is only right because they use the magazines for their purpose but contribute nothing.

WILLIAM: That's a wonderful thought.

Frances Steloff: Writers first started out in the magazines. The novels are put out on installment and then later gathered into a book. Hemingway first appeared in "This Quarter", Eliot began in "The Criterion". All the important writers have first appeared in magazines. I remember having a letter that Joyce wrote to his agent, thinking that nobody was interested in his work. Then Joyce appeared in "Transition" - think of all those "Transition" writers! How else? What other outlet did they have until they proved they could write.

Yet the magazine is not supported and has such a difficult time surviving. I always gave the magazines first row in the window, and the rest were always placed in front at the shop. Andreas Brown now puts them in back, which is terrible, I think. We quarreled about it all the time. I tried to get them back up front so that people can drop in and look them over. I know many people who come in for that.

So the publishers should be approached and pressed on this angle. They get the benefits. What's a few thousand dollars a year to them? They earn it back. They have scouts that they pay much more to find material.

Adele: Big publishers now are owned by huge companies to whom $3,000 can be written off easily as a tax loss. Maybe they'd even like to do that.

WILLIAM: There might be a danger though; they'd want to dominate them. Xerox was interested in buying "Voyages" three years ago, but I didn't even talk to them. They wanted the rights to put it on microfilm, which was okay, because they do that sort of thing, but then they wanted to put their own people in it. Xerox can get so many things but they couldn't get my magazine.

Adele: That is heroic...

Valerie: What do your writers and artists do to support themselves?

WILLIAM: Josephine Miles is an extraordinary woman. She is a professor of English at Berkeley, who has been a cripple all of her life and lives in a wheelchair. She writes absolutely beautiful poetry. Jane Cooper is a professor of English at Sarah Lawrence. Caroline Gordon writes wonderful novels. She was Alan Tate's wife. I published young writers. One was a young black high school girl from Texas. I didn't know who she was but just accepted her poem from the pile. The writers range. Most people who write for these magazines are not concerned about money. If they were they wouldn't send you anything in the first place. They simply know better. So it's not even a consideration.

ANAIS: I think that writers have accepted that there were two kinds of market; the literary and college magazines that can't pay and the commercial publishers.

WILLIAM: It would not hurt a young writer or artist or photographer to get in some magazines and develop a national reputation for their future work. I've tried to pay something from time to time. I do what I can. They benefit themselves by getting "credits" with the magazines.

Ann Roche: I don't want to get too personal, but do you have an independent income?

WILLIAM: I am, to this point in my life, still a bachelor which enables me to put some money into the magazine.

Ann Roche: Do you earn money from your own writings?

WILLIAM: No, I write poems, which don't bring in money. I have been gainfully employed all my life. I've been very lucky to have had interesting jobs.

As a little gift to everyone here I want to give you something I wrote in the midst of an interminable afternoon business meeting. I looked out over these buildings in Washington and their boxiness reminded me of the Soviet Union. It was February, and the sun started to come out at 3:15 in the afternoon. I wrote a poem right there on the spot while I was thinking of Anais Nin. I sent it to her and to "Nation Magazine", which published it. I have a copy of it for each one of you as a memento of this "furrawn":

THINKING OF ANAIS NIN

I dream of wayward gulls
and all landless lovers
Rare moments of winter sun
Peace, privacy, for everyone.

Evelyn Hinz: Mr. Claire, being in the position where you are reading the work of other writers, as well as being a writer yourself, and realizing that should you publish something, you will perhaps be giving this person his/her first start, and if you reject it, denying a talent, is fallibility a problem for an editor?

WILLIAM: Oh very much so. In Anais' *Diary,* or maybe in the *Novel of the Future,* she writes about how damaging this can be to a writer's reputation, especially a young writer. I have never sent a rejection slip without a little note, even though a lot of people send completely unsuitable things to the magazine, which gets discouraging. But I try not to hurt any feelings, because writing is an expression, after all, of something. I tell some people that they have the wrong magazine, that perhaps they might want to send their poem to Hallmark Cards or "McCall's."

Frances: I think that's a ticklish thing. You hate to encourage people to do something bad - bad poetry or bad anything - and you can't tell when or how they will develop, and so I think it's best to be honest with them, to tell them the truth and say, keep trying. I think that they have to be told that it's not good yet.

In The Poetry Society of America poems are read and judged anonymously, which helps. I think that we who have to make judgments should get to the point where we can tell writers that it's really not good poetry now, but keep on trying. Look at H.L. Mencken. He bought every copy of his first book of poems in order to destroy them. He paid high prices too. When we found out what he did with them, we stopped selling them to him.

Practice is good for writers; it builds their capacity to do better. I think many writers would develop into something good if given an opportunity. Writers need sympathetic readers more than they need food. I've always felt that, anyway. They have to have an audience. If not an audience, at least someone who will be interested in their work. And I always tried to meet that need.

Trew: Bill tries to respond to everyone in a way that will be helpful. He is gentle and giving, yet he speaks little of himself or of his inner feelings. He is a mystery. He also is a good balance here and represents man well.

56

Trew: I have trouble listening to her words because I keep seeing the searing pain in her eyes and I wonder what it is all about . . . She takes her role as critic and artist very seriously.

Adele: Her eyes are full of love and pain.

Joan: The first thing I notice about Evelyn Hinz is her bright dark eyes.

CHAPTER SEVEN

EVELYN J. HINZ: THE CREATIVE CRITIC

Evelyn Hinz is from a family of 16 children. She is tall, beautiful, and aloof. Her critical studies have appeared in "The D. H. Lawrence Reveiw", "Genre", "Contemporary Literature", "Bucknell Review", "Studies in the Novel" and elsewhere, but her importance for us is in having authored the first complete study of all the published works by Anais Nin in a book called **The Mirror and the Garden**. *She had been in touch with Swallow Press, when she had completed the book manuscript, but just at that time Alan Swallow died and the Press underwent a transition of ownership. It was at Alan Swallow's funeral that William Claire met Anais Nin. Thus, another circle of friendship, which had begun long before, was brought out at this Weekend.*

Presently Evelyn Hinz is a Post-Doctoral Fellow at the University of Manitoba, Winnepeg, Canada. Among other things, she is preparing for publication an edited version of Anais Nin's past lectures.

Evelyn Hinz: My role here today is that of critic. I would like to speak on behalf of the critic because I think generally there is an ingrained feeling that critics cannot be free poeple, that artists are on one side and critics on the other, and that the critic is a parasite on the artist, that the critic is not pure in his / her own right.

Now, before I came here, "Contemporary Literature" came out, wherein I have a review of Anais' 4th volume of the **Diary.** This volume, as you know, describes Nin's battle with the critics, particularly Edmund Wilson. I think the reason for the bad odor that critics have is partly a result of the problem that Nin herself explores in that volume of **The Diary**, which is the idea that the critic is supposed to be a kind of computer, sitting down and saying what this is all about; tearing a work of art apart and reducing it to the things it came from is a favorite critical past time called "source hunting". We have too many people going through Nin's **Diaries** and fiction, saying, "Now do you know who this person is and how this incident came about?" To me, this is the worst kind of reductivism because this denies the artist the ability to take his/her experience and shape it.

I want to give you some idea of the kind of criticism I hope I represent. As I read Nin's fiction, I responded by thinking, "there's nothing like this." And suddenly I was forced to ask, "If I responded, why did I respond and where did the unusualness of her writing lie?" In the introduction to one of her books, Harry T. Moore wrote, "Anais Nin virtually invented a type of novel. To say this is not to say her books of fiction cannot be read like any others, but rather it is said to emphasize her originality." The question that came to my mind is, "Can you read Nin's fiction like you can read other fiction, can you approach her work like you approach the traditional novel of the 18th and 19th century?" I came to the conclusion that you couldn't. And, therefore, when you use the term **novel** to describe Nin's works you are really up against a problem because the word **novel** carries certain connotations.

When we think of a novel we think of one thing in particular and that's characters in a social setting. Always the emphasis is upon social context and how individuals exist in that context. The individuals are measured — whether or not they measure up. So we always have a social scene in mind. Some of the modern novelists, maybe as a result of Anais' influence, have been moving away from this toward her type of fiction. The question became then, if social character is what a novel is concerned with, what do we think of when we pick up one of Nin's works? It came to my mind that whereas when you read a novel and say it's a story about this and this and this, when you pick up, for example, **A Spy in the House of Love**, we say one thing: "Sabina". If we pick up **Ladders to Fire** we say "Lillian" or "Djuna". And if we look a little more closely, what we see is Nin concerned with character — character first, and then society as it involves that character — as that character is involved.

This led me to consider why is this difference and where does this difference originate? Why do we have Nin focusing upon character and other novelists upon the individual in a social setting? I think I found the answer in her little pamphlet called "Realism and Reality." According to Nin, reality reflects what the individual sees; whereas because of scientific conditioning most of us think that reality is the objective photographic fact of life. According to Nin, the world is there, but each of us sees the world as it affects the person which determines how the person will act out her life. Furthermore, as Nin dramatizes in her fiction so frequently, the social roles we play very frequently are disguises, which we put on so that we don't have to reveal what we are really like because we are afraid, afraid we won't be acceptable.

Sometimes if this goes on for a long enough time we simply become social figures, and no longer recognize what we really feel and consequently become very frustrated, anxious people, blaming our environment. We say if we had a better system, then we'd be happy. Anais Nin's whole point is, before we can change anything, we've got to understand what we really are like, what do we really want? So when we say that Nin's fiction is unique we do not simply mean that she makes an innovation within the novel form but actually that she questions the form of the novel, the whole orientation towards being objective. This is the reason for the difference between her fiction and the kind of thing you usually read.

I'd like now to talk about the novels, about some of the characters, how her point of view makes for the kind of style that she writes. When we were talking yesterday, most of you mentioned that you had read the **Diaries** but a couple of you told me that you had a little difficulty reading her fiction. Now here I had a fortunate experience in many ways. When I started working on Nin the **Diaries** weren't out so there was only the fiction. So I approached the fiction and came to terms with the fiction itself and discovered this theme of "realism and reality" with the aid of her little discussion in the pamphlet. When the **Diaries** came out, I was, of course, very anxious to read them because my concern was what was she going to say in the **Diary** and how was it going to be related to what I had interpreted as her message and major themes and techniques in her fiction. Then when **The Novel of the Future** came out with her critical theory, I had a double fit. Now surely the first part of my book was going to be ruined because she would say something that's contrary to what I discovered.

I hope I speak correctly when I say that **Novel of the Future** confirmed what I had discovered rather than in any way forced me to alter it. The format that I set up in my book, **The Mirror and the Garden**, was to use my interpretations of the novel and her themes and characters and then go to **The Novel of the Future** and look back. That's why I call the chapter "Looking Backwards" to see wherein we came to the same perceptions. Now the reason I bring this up specifically is because I want to point out that I came to Nin's work when there was nothing to rely on but intuition and response. There were no books written on her at that time. The articles that were written called her unrealistic. I found myself in the position of saying, "Well if I responded, what am I responding to, am I being unrealistic?" And I didn't think I was unrealistic. I thought I was very realistic. So consequently I was forced to define for myself, at the same time that I explained her themes, where my stand was. So, what Nin's fiction did was force me to say what I believed in, and what my attitude toward reality was. I think this is essentially one of the great values of Nin's writing, that she does force you to ask yourself this question.

I should think that we could call Nin's books "character studies" rather than "novels" because in a typical novel, as we were saying earlier, something happens, whereas in Nin's work we begin with the character and with that point of view. We are not given a story about how she went shopping and then met this marvelous young man and this kind of thing. Rather, the only thing that appears in one of Nin's works is whatever that character happens to be driven to seeing at that time, and only in the way she sees it. Consequently all the characters, the minor characters in Nin's works, are there not as fully drawn figures but rather in terms of defining what the central character is thinking and her attitudes. **A Spy in the House of Love** is beautiful in that way because we have Sabina and five different men. What we get is Sabina's point of view of each of these, which, because of her very needs may not necessarily give a fully drawn character.

In each of Nin's works there is a dialogue between the character's social self and inner feelings, and the conflict between them. So that in her works instead of a progressive movement of a plot, there is this dramatic struggle of the character trying to come to terms with herself, and because Nin dwells consistently in the mind, sometimes there is no resolution. This happens very frequently, for example, in the cases of Stella, Sabina, Djuna and Lillian; there is more in the case of Djuna and Lillian, during which we readers come to some kind of a reconciliation of their roles. So, I think if we approach Nin's fiction by saying at the beginning, now I'm not going to make any expectations, I am simply going to respond and realize that this is a character, that we want to meet this character, then the difficulites begin to dissolve.

Think how in our own lives things happen very quickly and we don't take into account anything except the things that happen to ourselves. This is the kind of a movement you see in these fictions. We can move from one place to another very rapidly. And the reason we do is that the mind, of course, the subconscious, is not limited as we are physically to a geographical location and movement.

Another way I think of approaching Nin's fiction that would be very helpful is to have someone read it to you. Nin's work is essentially poetic and her use of language is supposed to generate an emotional rather than intellectual reaction. So if you have difficulty getting into a work, I suggest you simply ask someone to read it to you. Somehow when we hear someone speaking we allow ourselves to go along with what's being said, whereas when we are sitting down reading, we've been accustomed to being told exactly where we're going and how. When we listen to the words we hear how Nin proceeds.

Let me give you an example: Take any one of her works. Immediately you realize that you are dealing with a different kind of reality to which you have to respond emotionally rather than intellectually. From **Seduction of the Minotaur**:

> Some writers have their inception in the blueprint of a dream, some in the urgency of contradicting a dream. Lillian's recurrent dream of a ship that could not reach the water, that sailed laboriously, pushed by her with great effort, through city street, had determined her course toward the sea, as if she would give this ship, once and for all its proper sea bed.
> She had landed in the city of Golconda where the sun painted everything with gold, the lining of her thoughts, the warm valises, the plain beetles, Golconda of the golden age, the golden aster, the golden eagle, the golden goose, the golden fleece, the golden robin, the goldenrod, the golden seal, the golden warbler, the golden wattles, the golden wedding, and the gold fish, and the gold of pleasure, the gold stone, the gold thread, the fool's gold.
> With the first swallow of air she inhaled a drug of forgetfulness well known to adventurers.

Suddenly you are set off and not making any demands anymore. Whereas, if Nin had said Lillian was born in 1932, her father was named Mr. Smith and since she was not getting along very well with her husband, she decided to go away, you see that we're in an entirely different realm.

Now as I said, I responded to Nin and wrote what I believed in terms of what she believed. If we approach fiction not as something dead but as something alive, then we should be able to have as great and personal a response to a book as we do to another human being. What the artist does is to create something out of her own experience her response to experience. What the critic does, the creative critic, is to create something out of the response to what the artist has done. In both cases we are working with response, with a personal response. And in this sense I think criticism can be as creative as can the work of art itself. All we've changed is the medium of expression.

The artist works directly with the experience and I, as critic, work with Nin's books. Through criticism I express myself as I attempt to explain what her works mean. I might read her works entirely differently from someone else. I could try to be very objective and say I'm only going to count the images here or number of lines, and so forth. Then, of course, I wouldn't have become involved. When I defend Nin's practice, for example, and suggest that I agree that realism is a faulty concept and that reality does lie in the individual perception, then I'm expressing my own convictions. Now if I'm an academic critic, and I don't like Nin, what I'll do is write pejorative work or else I won't touch her. Or, I'll rationalize and say I don't like her because she's unrealistic. Then the question to ask is, 'unrealistic according to whose standard'? Because, unfortunately, we have been programmed to believe that the photograph, science, and statistics constitute the real thing; consequently we try to measure ourselves up to these things with disastrous results. We have emotional lives and we have to admit them and make the most of them.

So I think that the value of Nin then for the artist in particular is that she makes you ask yourself, "Are you really working in an old medium, a worn out mold, or do you recognize the organic significance of the mold in which you're working?" She's questioning the very medium that you're working in just as she rejected the novel format because it reflected a different orientation. The artist should ask herself, "Am I merely reproducing something that has been done, or am I really creating something?" And creation stems from where you place your values.

The second question that I think Nin brings out and makes all of us face is the question of social responsibility. We hear so much these days about the critic and the artist being socially responsible. Indeed when I showed the first draft of my study of her works to a colleague, he said, "Not only is she irresponsible but you're promoting her irresponsibility."

But, Nin asks, "What is **social responsibility**?" Before society can be put into order, the individual has to be put in order. Otherwise, simply what we are doing is rationalizing our own inadequacies rather than asking where does the inadequacy itself reside. Because, after all, society is only made up of individuals. And consequently to evoke or suggest a change in platform and to believe this is going to change the human being is entirely naive.

This relates to the mirror image, which I brought to the title of my book. What Nin wants to do is get, as she says, to the roots. What are the roots of the matter? So in each of her works of fiction this is what she is looking for specifically. What is the natural character before civilization imposed a form upon it? And in making us ask this question, that is, to consider what we believe social reality and responsibility to be, I think Nin provides a corrective today. She especially makes us examine when we pay allegiance to a political movement whether we understand ourselves before we decide on this move. Are we simply compensating for a problem of our own or do we really believe this means is going to be the most effective solution?

Now with respect to her **Diary** itself, I'd like to point out what I think is unique. Nin doesn't write down things in the **Diary** simply because they happened during the day, nor to collect facts for future stories. If you read her **Diaries** you realize her writing down everything is in order to find out, "Who am I? Why did this particular thing appeal to me? What does that reveal about me?" In **House of Incest,** you remember, she begins one of her chapters — "Does anyone know who I am?" We can give our social answers: My name is Evelyn Hinz and I work at the University. But that's not me, that's the kind of clothes I happen to be wearing today. What's going to happen if I take the mask off or am I ready to take the mask off?

The second thing about Nin's writing the **Diary** is that she writes down not just the incident but does it immediately so she eopresses her response before she has time to become self-conscious about it. The great value of that writing, of course, is not only that it keeps you writing every day but that you are spontaneous about it. It's different from sitting down to write a book and describing an incident with all the craft you can. Yet the experience that is written spontaneously can still be retrieved for a story. But it has not been couched in an artificial form or forced into a certain mold.

This brings me to a question I would like to ask you, Anais, if it would be all right? Since your **Diary** has become public and widely known, do you find that you still write a diary?

Anais Nin: This year I haven't, in all honesty, because of the nature of my correspondence. It was like an addition to the **Diary** or an answer to it. I would receive diaries from others. They were not letters; they were parts of diaries. I felt that answering them might be for the moment the natural flowering of the diary. There would be a dialogue between **Diary** and confessional letters and personal letters. So I stopped this year but I'm not sure that that is the final metamorphosis. Once the **Diary** is opened and shared, it seemed there should be an answer.

Evelyn Hinz: Do you think the fact that you now know that your **Diary** is being published will affect your writing?

Anais: No, because I kept the secret **so** long. I had such a habit of secrecy from the age of 11 until the time that I published it — a long time — that I believe in my power to keep a secret. I tell others that what I write today nobody will want to see, which helps me to maintain that continuity and truthfulness. I would like to ask you a question. Why, since the **Diaries** have come out, do people understand the fiction? I am not sure that I understand why reading the **Diaries** makes the fiction clearer.

Evelyn Hinz: In the **Diary** people can see the character or the incident you are describing in a context. I think it was the fact that you said you are working in the world of the dream, the edifice without dimension, in your fiction that caused an uneasy feeling. One doesn't know where to begin, where exactly one is.

Anais: So the **Diary** gave them...?

Evelyn: Context. In a way the **Diary** is the medium between both old and new writing. It has the qualities of a novel but it also has the realities of the old way of writing. The **Diary** is a bridge of understanding to the novels.

Anais: Did the **Diary** persuade everyone that I was a realist?

Evelyn: I think it gave them a context for the unusualness of your fiction.

Anais: Fiction was a destination. They were missing elements which the **Diary** filled in. Then they could believe it.

Adele: To me, as a painter, I think the fiction was very related to the creation of painting. A natural kind of thing, as in a painting you leave this out or that out to build an image. That's the same kind of process that people aren't used to seeing in writing.

Evelyn: That's right. Anais has used that image of her writing as the canvas, saying... The missing elements on the half empty canvas were important because they were the only space in which the human imagination could draw its own images.

You see, what Anais is trying to do in fiction is to allow you to come with your whole emotional subconscious response too. Now if she describes your characters or gives you too concrete a setting, you would know automatically that you couldn't fit in there because your house happens to be blue and this one happens to be green, that syndrome. But leaving spaces out, pursuing just the essentials, allows the reader to fill in the gaps with her own responses and identification.

*Daisy Aldan: I think a person who was accustomed to reading and writing poetry would respond immediately to the novels and not need the **Diaries** as a bridge. But a person has to learn the language of poetry, which Anais' fiction is. The **Diaries** were an illumination of the distilled and concise language of the novels, the poetic prose that was more difficult to understand.*

Evelyn Hinz: That's true. The words 'poetic novel' are very good, except that there are so many built-in connotations of what the word 'novel' means that I'd like to throw the term out altogether. Somehow in the convention of prose fiction, rather than poetry, we demand to know exactly where we are. Of course the novel started in the 18th century as history.

Anais Nin: Do you remember how Dreiser wrote about what the characters paid for rent, how old they were, where they lived, what street...?

Evelyn: Not only that, he described in **Sister Carrie**, a very exciting getaway. The characters have stolen a lot of money and are rushing for the train which is to leave in five minutes, and all of a sudden, one of them makes a phone call from a telephone booth. Dreiser spends three pages describing the telephone booth, how it was the first in America, and I'm sure that if the character was really trying to catch this train he missed it!

Elaine Streitfield: People say there is no reality in Nin's interior writing, but artists and poets have long felt that the deeper reality is in the interior of a person.

Moira Collins: What I always thought was that people who do not think she deals with reality feel threatened by her because they do not face their interior lives. They prefer to relegate her as unreal.

Anais: A person is not alive without emotional reality, which is feeling what is happening to me. I never spoke of escaping reality, I simply spoke of the relation of our beings to our emotional reality.

Beatrice Harris: Where does the emotional reality develop? From something external which elicits emotion within you, so they're connected. It isn't that one has an emotional reality without the external reality. They're there together, inter-acting.

Daisy Aldan: People sometimes get the impression that Anais just lets exquisite language flow out of her. I think her lasting value as an artist is her skill with words and imagery. Her craft is not just automatic writing, but involves a tremendous conscious effort and intelligence in working the feelings into an integral part of the work. One of the great and almost indefinable things of her work is the style, which comes through even in foreign languages.

Evelyn: Proust said that style is not a matter of technique but of vision. I think Anais suggests that the emotions direct how our perceptions are formed. Henry Miller thought that everything should be written down as it came and not given artistic form or polish. In the first volume of the **Diary** Anais says that things have to be cut in order to produce gems. I see her fiction as work of art in this sense.

In The Novel of the Future the first chapter begins, "Proceed from the dream outward." You have to begin with an understanding of what you are like but to remain disoriented from the world is to her most unfortunate. Earlier today Valerie asked Anais whether she intended not to have her women characters find fulfillment in their work. Anais made the point that in the fiction she was exploring women who had problems, not ones who had resolved their problems. In presenting Sabina, Lillian, Djuna, and Stella, Nin is not saying this is the way all women are, unresolved in their conflicts, but that these are some of the conflicts that women have to come to terms with.

Anna Balakian: Actually in French, the word for novel, 'roman' comes from the word 'romance', which means prose written in the vernacular as opposed to things written about unreality. Therefore, it is a very appropriate word because it means that it is about life — reality, not realism — the total reality of this earth in opposition to spiritual writings about another earth or world, metaphysical world.

Anais: But the word 'novel' in English is taken from the Italian 'novella', meaning "the never experienced before." So we have two sources for the novel.

Anna Balakian: When you go through the history of the novel right through the 19th century which was supposed to be realistic, the novels of that era did create a relationship between the subjective and the objective. Even today, what remains of Zola is the fact that for moments he was a poet. If he had followed strictly the theories of the naturalistic novel, he'd be dead as a doornail the way some of the others who followed him and his precepts, rather than his realizations, have died.

Daisy Aldan: The naturalistic novel is out of favor because it is false. People now in their developing consciousness are beginning to realize that the human being is not just a physical body but an entity, a balanced entity between the spiritual and physical. People see that the physical body is an empty shell, a corpse, without the feelings and strivings, the other side of human nature, to fill and balance it.

Evelyn Hinz: It is significant that the artists and the young people have become Nin's favorite audience. The young people are not yet acclimatized to their social roles and the artists have always recognized that we need more than a mirror of ourselves in terms of realism.

Adele: I felt Evelyn's effort to be able to speak like that in front of a group. Her passionate interest in Anaïs gave her the strength, not ego. She became lost in her talk, radiated and transcended her subject. Evelyn seemed to me deeply passionate but all inside. She was like looking at hot lava pressing against strong transparent walls of lucite. Everything contained, nothing spilled over, but I could see all the surging.

CHAPTER EIGHT

DAISY ALDAN: BOOKS AND THE LIVING HAND

Daisy Aldan is a Poet, Publisher, and Teacher. Her books include: **Seven:Seven, Destruction of Cathedrals and Other Poems, Breakthrough, Love Poems by Daisy Aldan.** *She has published the works of poets, artists, and musicians in her many* **Folder Editions** *and translated the work of poets, such as Stephen Mallarme's* **Un Coup de Dés** *and Albert Steffen's* **Selected Poems.**

In stature she is small and sturdy, possessed of dignity and energy. She wears an elegant velvet vest with silk appliqué, which she bought from one of the weekenders, Sas Colby. She stands before us near a table overflowing with books that she had brought out, the scope of which suddenly seems to surprise her as her talk unfolds. She has two voices, one of practicality, the other of poetic drama. As she speaks, she fairly dances!

DAISY ALDAN: One of my aims is to encourage and teach people to work with imagination through the living hand, because there is something pretty wonderful that emanates from the work that the living hand has touched. Often IBM machines are being used to reproduce mass quantities of books and I know that I for one can always tell when an IBM machine has set the type. I'm not against the machine. I don't feel we should go backwards to the ancient methods, but we have to control the machine and use it when it is appropriate. When you want distribution in wide circles, use an IBM machine. But creative work is a different matter. So it is one of my missions to do as much as possible to bring back hand quality to the work.

For eighteen years I've been involved with designing, publishing, distributing, writing invoices, reading, walking into bookstores with books and so forth. I began as editor of my literary magazine in college. After college in 1946, when I was teaching and had a girl in my class who was good with calligraphy, I thought it would be nice to put my poems in calligraphy. Frances Steloff was the first one to take this book. (She demonstrates how it was made from wallpaper and pasted laundry cardboard sheets. Throughout her talk she shows samples of her books.) I did about 500 of these. You must always remember that the more copies you do, the cheaper it becomes. A few years ago I had all the extras in a friend's attic and she said, "What shall I do with them?"

I said, "Throw them out."

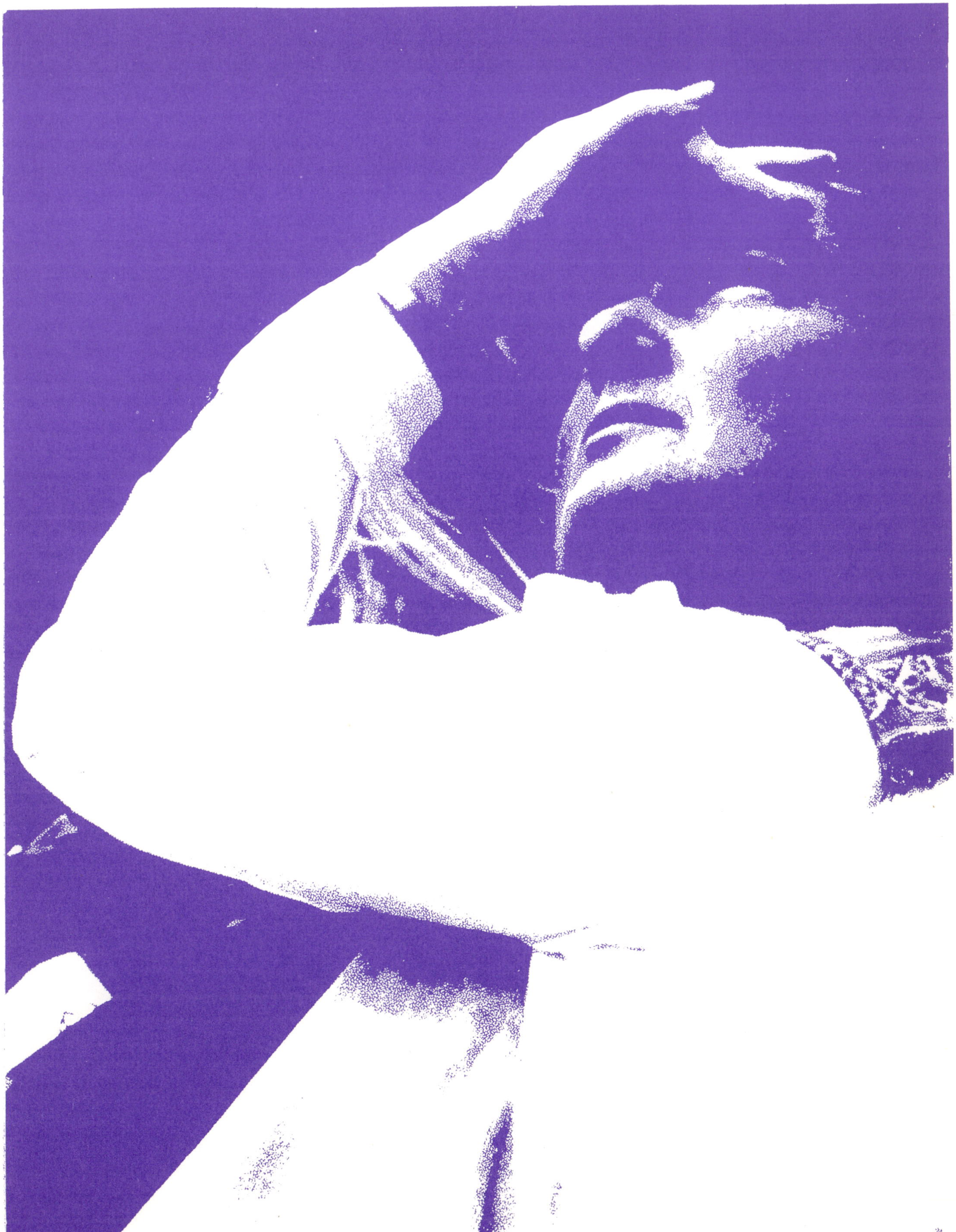

That week I received a telephone call from Boston from a book dealer, Henry Wenning, who asked, "Where can I get a few copies of your first book? There are some people who are collecting your books."

And I thought, "My God, I've just thrown away thousands of dollars." You never know. Big business, disgusting as it is, is now commercializing manuscripts.

As I look back, I can see that at that particular time a literary life began which changed the course of my life. I was working on a doctorate thesis on **The Influence of French Surrealism on American Literature.** *I didn't know destiny would bring me here with three people that affected my life then. One is Frances Steloff, who encouraged my first book, the other is Anna Balakian who agreed to be on my doctorate committee at NYU when I was told by other people at the school that it was too early to write about Surrealism. And here is Anais. Three people who really, at certain turning points in my life appeared. They are all here. I can't believe that this is coincidence!*

I came into contact with many poets through that dissertation topic. You know, you ray out something that starts moving things in your direction which weren't moving before. I found that continuously. I came into contact with young unknown poets who since became major poets in America and painters who were unable to get their work exhibited. One was Grace Hartigan, who was at the time calling herself George Hartigan so she could get her work exhibited. She ultimately became one of the most important Abstract Expressionist painters. Others were Frank O'Hara, John Ashbery, Kenneth Koch. These were all young unpublished poets. The so-called academic poets were in the saddle, and if you had written anything that was different in style or form, you could not get your work published. At the time there were 40 literary magazines in America and now there must be 400,000 from what I see in the Gotham Book Mart. And **View,** *which had been publishing the older surrealist poets, was discontinued, so I said to myself, that I'd like to publish a magazine for the works of these friends of mine.*

I also was writing in that style. In fact, at the time I didn't know that people would call my work 'surrealist' because I was not influenced by the Surrealists. I thought, 'Well, I'll steal paper from school and make a little magazine.' When I got to work, I found that my taste in paper was too fine. I chose the most expensive laid paper that you could find, because I loved the way it felt. The visual is part of the poetic experience and a beautiful book is just as important as the contents. To hold a book, to see it - the paper it is on - the way the type is arranged on the page - is really a total experience.

I perhaps was influenced by Mallarmé who also thought the visual aspect of a poem was important. I had translated the **Coup de Dés,** *because I was terrribly interested in avant garde poetry. I found out later that Gide had called this the most untranslatable poem in any language! One of Mallarme's precepts was that the appearance of the poem on the pages was an integral part of the experience because there is the heard poem and there is the written poem. When you see the written poem and hear it with an inner ear, these are two different experiences. The heard poem is not the written poem. I felt that way too and wanted the whole book to be a beautiful artistic work.*

That was my downfall. I had paper but when I searched for a cheap printer, I did not realize that the printer's union pays high school graduates $350 a week.

I said, "Oh, my God, that's too much for me." My teaching salary was quite low. Yet, I ended up paying for this and subsequent books myself. Somebody asked yesterday (this morning seems like days ago!) - if Bill Claire had an income? He said, "No," and I had to smile because I'm often asked that question, and I never have either. I'm a slave of the classroom because I've never had an independent income. But I've used the money the same way people buy fur coats. But I want to urge you not to feel that you are depriving yourself of other things because it will bring you back untold wealth in other ways.

I found that I could not afford to have my work done by a professional printer, so as Anais did, I looked through a catalogue that sold presses and ordered a press to be sent to me through the mail with type. I never took a course in book production but through necessity I learned. I looked through books of type and decided on Vogue type because of its new quality. I have since become more traditional in the type I use. But this I wanted to be avant garde, you know, sans serif type. It was interesting that later when I sent Anais **Folder 1** *she wrote back and said that because I was using the same type she had, she wondered if I had bought her type. It was one of those strange coincidences!*

I had a big case of letters, which I started putting together in a chase. I made many errors and I went through a lot of pain - everything was filthy with printer's ink. **Folder 1** *is now a collector's item which I can't afford to buy back because every one in it is well known and it was done by hand.*

So in the process of making the **Folders,** *first I had to get manuscripts, then I had to figure out how it was going to be bound. Bindings are much more expensive than printers. I couldn't afford it, so I started* *designing how to do it so the pages wouldn't fall out, and I conceived, after many trials and errors, a folder form. And then I thought, "How wonderful! Now I can give each poet four pages for him/herself." I tried to think of a title. The first was going to be, "Any Minute Now, Somebody's Going to Do It." That was too long and pretentious. So were the names of other magazines, like "Kaleidoscope", "Spectrum", "Rainbow", "Prism". I said, "No, if I'm going to do it this way, let's simply call it **Folder**." And that's how we got the name.*

*I spent hours cutting out the forms, scoring and folding, because I didn't know that you could go to somebody who could make a mold and chop all the sheets into shape in one operation. Then there was the printing, after which the poets and I collated everything on a big table. At the same time I had been puttering around with making a silk screened Christmas card, which technique I eventually used in my crowning glory of publishing. My idea was to include painters' work in the **Folders** too. I always really wanted to bring the whole media together - painting, poetry, and music. I had musicians like Ned Rorem and Ben Weber, who took poems of people like Frank O'Hara's and put them to music. I was very ambitious without being commercially ambitious.*

I got a little loft known as The Studio, where I brought my printing press and papers, which became the center for all these young poets and painters. These avant gardists were starting what was later to become the Abstract Expressionist school. At that time DeKooning was selling paintings for $50, which today are worth $50,000. I really intended to buy one but didn't find the time. If I had, I probably now could retire and publish books!

Adele: How many were in your first editions?

DAISY: Five hundred in **Folder 1.** *They are hard to find now but at that time I had a hard time selling them for 50c.*

Things find their way into the world. The quality of the writers received attention from the literary world. If you publish a book or a magazine, the first thing to do is to bring a bunch to the Gotham Book Mart, of course! There were reviews in "The New York Times" and so forth. Once a book is started - if it has any worth - it will find its way. Don't ever be afraid to start something. Don't think that it's vanity publishing. Anais, Edgar Allen Poe, Virginia Woolf, Proust, Rimbaud, all published their work first. If it's good, it's not vanity. It's only vanity publishing if it's bad. Besides, commercial publishers do terrible things to your work.

*When I came to doing **Folder II**, I knew that I could not possibly set type again, letter by letter, so I learned about linotype. Linotype is* *arranging lines of type on a page instead of words. You still create by putting lines and spaces where you want them. Someone warned me not to let anyone know I was doing this because women were not allowed in the Printers' Union and I could get a fine. I think I was the only female linotype setter in New York at the time. I secretly put my* **Folder** *together.*

I used photography and serigraphs by painters. In **Folder III** *I used a more elaborate cover done by Grace Hartigan. I published translations from different poets. I think I was the first one to publish George Seferis in this country. I had a whole group of Greek, Haitian and Italian poets. I was the first one to publish Peir Paolo Pasolini here, who has subsequently become known as a filmmaker also. The* **Folder's** *name was spreading out. I got to know Alice B. Toklas and Princess Marguerite Caetani. One day I visited Anais and there was Caresse Crosby. I considered her Black Sun Press fantastic. Here was a woman who blished beautiful books by writers no one ever heard of. I'm sure Anna Balakian had known about these people long before I did. But, do you see how one person inspires another? That's why we have to work together and inspire each other. It is very important for the world today that we do this.*

In **Folder IV**, *I took the opportunity to put out my translations of Mallarmé's* **Coup de Dés,** *which had never been able to get printed the way he wanted it printed. That's why I say, go ahead and do your own things. Commercial publishers will never do them your way. Mallarmé wanted it done on music sheets because it was structured like a symphony. The original version also has no punctuation and the grammer, the syntax, seems to be mixed up but that's all part of the poem. I with my linotype and great love brought one of his greatest poems to existence.*

Remember, this work in the **Folder** *by these wonderful talented musicians, poets and painters, I couldn't sell for a dollar. Some people said, "Give it away to friends." You must never do it for money because it is impossible to make money. Imagine a dollar for all that!*

When **Folder IV** *came out, I felt that the mission of my magazine was over. Now I was ready for my crowning glory. We took four of the poets and four painters and decided that we would put out four bound books. We had a big silk screen in the studio and paints. These books are really* **books of art.** *They consist of poems and serigraphs. You can tell that the painting is not reproduced by machine, because you can feel it. The poems were printed in Germany. We found that you could get cheaper paper and binding there. It took ages for it to come back but it was worth it. After that I decided to put out a book a year. Several* *of my friends said I was becoming known as an editor, not a poet, that I too must have a book. But I made a number for friends anyway, if I felt the poems were good enough. With an exquisite photographer, I did a book of my own called* **Seven:Seven; Photographs and Poems.** *Then a couple of years ago I had a poem "Journey" put into calligraphy. I met all kinds of calligraphers and in a matter of a few weeks did a whole series.*

Someone: What do you sell **Or Learn to Walk On Water** *for?*

DAISY: $150.00. I also put it out in a cheap offset edition. All these were very well received.

When I was in Switzerland I translated the Swiss poet Albert Steffen and put out a book of his poems. My book, **Breakthrough,** *was printed in Switzerland where I was able to arrange the type and page by hand. There were two American commercial publishers interested in this but I withdrew the book because they wanted to put it out in a cheap paperback and these poems must be done this way, laid out according to spaces, because that is an integral part of the poem.*

Now I just want to briefly go over the steps in publishing you would have to take. First, get a manuscript you want to publish, whether it's yours or a friend's; arrange it the way you want, and decide what kind of book you want and what kind of process you want to use - handwriting, calligraphy, linotype or wood blocks - there are all kinds of ways. Then decide on what paper you want; get linotype made or do calligraphy and drawings. Make a little dummy so that when someone's printing it, he or she knows what to do. Paste up the pages after you get your type or your printing. You must be careful because it will come out just the way you paste it. It can't be crooked, so work with rulers. Then get a printer and then you will get galleys to correct. Send them back to the printer and when it's printed, find somebody to bind it in boards and cloth. The next process is the distributing of the work. (She kicks her foot into the air). **GO AHEAD AND DO IT.**

Daisy's books are eagerly examined and discussed by the participants. Then Anais Nin comes forward and unlocks a glass cabinet, in which her hand-printed editions, bearing the imprint of Gemor Press, have been on display. As she talks, she passes around her books.
ANAIS: *Now for an inspirational story after all the technicalities. When I came from France in 1940 I had three books to be done and couldn't get any publisher. I bought a second hand press with $100 loaned by Ms. Steloff. We got a place on MacDougall Street in such an old house that when you put the press on the floor it began to sway. It was a hand press that was operated like a sewing machine with your foot. I had two people help me set up the book. One was Gonzalo whom I*

wrote about in **The Diary** and the other one was a cousin who doesn't wish to be named. We learned from an instruction book. It said to oil the rollers, so we put oil on the rollers and as a result we couldn't print for a whole week!

It took me eight months to hand set **Winter of Artifice,** and being a novice I never learned to properly space words. In one place I separated the word "love", of course to the delight of the critics. Then I did **Under a Glass Bell,** by hand. We used the Blake method of printing from copper plates done by the artist, Ian Hugo. Each one of these had to be pulled individually. Then we had to wipe out the ink and put on another plate, a great deal of labor. The books took about a year to do. It took so long I finally realized that I wouldn't write if I went on.

Originally the press had been meant to be a collective press. We thought we would all work on it and do each other's books. Robert Duncan came and left his poems for me to do, so it ended up not being a collective press. After doing my stories, we finally did the very large book, **House of Incest,** also with real engravings pulled on an engraving press.

Of course I took these books to the Gotham Book Mart. They have since become collectors' items. I'm the only writer who wept when she had a contract with a commercial publisher because I thought now the books are going to look dull. I had to do it though because printing was a full time job, and I wanted to write.

Since this part of the Weekend is considered a workshop on the more unusual and artistic ways of putting books together, other persons are prepared to show what they have done.

Adele Aldridge describes her books. First she removes a very large beautiful book from its leather burlap portfolio. The book is hand-bound in burlap with an embroidered title. It contains hand-rubbed woodcut prints on double-folded rice paper. The prints are her interpretations of **I Ching** *hexagrams, in which she has created her eight basic symbols and inter-related them in sixty-four ways. Since the book would be very expensive for others to buy, she decided to make only two of them.*

As she was experimenting graphically with words, in a development from using words ironically, such as Pray/Pay, in her paintings, she made a large collection of visual word statements. These she called **Notpoems** *and produced them in three ways. Her first step was to hand-bind ten sets, each with its own unique and elegant cloth cover. Then she made* *cloth-covered box forms for ten more sets. Finally, she had printed a larger, less-expensive limited edition of the work, for which she designed and executed a binding of glossy paper and metal rings.*

Her most recent effort is a new color version of her **I Ching** *images. She hand-printed each page on a foot-treadle letter press, which required several run-throughs for each color used. Each page also required typesetting sentences selected from the* **I Ching,** *which she used to complement each print. To make 55 copies of this edition took her 5-1/2 months. To bind together each set of prints in a complete work of art she chose a transparent rose-colored plexiglass, for its affinity with the content and because its fire-like glow made you want to pick it up. Each volume she sells for $80.*

She describes herself as "obsessed with books", a term which would apply to all those creating books in this way. We have already been surprised to hear that Georgiana Peacher is silk-screening a novel. She shows us some of the 250 signatures that, when finished, will be divided and boxed in four folios. Her words are hand-lettered in different colors, each of which requires using a separate screen in the complicated process of preparing each page. Each page, furthermore, is designed in unusual arrangements of words on paper, often blended with images, all intended to build the meaning of this experimental "symphony" in prose, entitled **Mary Stuart's Ravishment Descending Time.** *It is a complex work of art, taking years to complete. It is her first book to print.*

Adele: I am moved by Georgiana, who is warm and shy and shows us her lovely work - a beautiful unfolding - who tells us that after years and years of work she quit her job one day to do what she wanted to do. I feel such identity with that, and such strength when I hear people throw things away, saying 'yes' to themselves.

Moira Collins shows a sample of her hand-written, "commonplace" books. She chooses her material with her personal response as the only guide. She says, a "commonplace" book is needed...

> **if you're carrying Ferlinghetti's line, "I hear America singing in the yellow pages" in your head and don't want to forget it; or if a friend's dream has an incredible parallel to an old Bella Coola myth you once read and you want to remember the connection. Often, one of the truest places of all is in one's mind, but if your mind is very opal and you find it hard to keep a diary or daily record, you might wish to write yourself out in a personal journal in which passages literary excerpts and comments form a sort of associative shorthand of how you were at a particular moment.**

She often makes such a book around a certain theme for favored individuals.

Another work, shown by Elaine Streitfeld has only been shared with her closest friends before now. It is a sheaf of pages containing one line narration with water colors and drawings, a childhood reminiscence entitled "Ah, The Beautiful Fragrance of Lime Blossoms in Florence Angela's Backyard". After hearing the others in the workshop, she feels inspired to turn the work into a complete book with her own magic hands.

The intense feelings from all the creativity witnessed during the day spill over during a festive dinner of animated talk and a round of toasts with wine. Nadine says, **I never did come to the table to eat but for the company.** *And Joan Anacreon shares a poem she made up on the spot:*

> Yes!
> Yes Yes Yes Yes!
> Yes to new places, new faces, to Spring
> Yes to painting and writing and flings
> Yes to today, the sun and tonight
> Yes to tomorrow, to ideas in flight
> to new friends, to new feelings
> to good times and good dealings
> Yes to living and giving
> to life
> Yes Yes Yes Yes!
> Oh Yes.

76

CHAPTER NINE

ANAIS NIN: EXCERPTS FROM THE **DIARY**

It is night, yet in the library lights cast a soft, relaxing glow around the room. People settle themselves comfortably on the cushions of couches or chairs. They are well-nourished, still aflame from the wine. Anais is to read to us. She sits before us quietly chatting, wearing a long, sleek gown, looking very lovely. We wait, preparing for the pleasure of hearing her voice bring to life her work. If this Weekend can be compared to a work of art itself, then as Adele says:

ANAIS IS THE CANVAS, WITHOUT WHICH THE PAINT CANNOT HOLD. SHE IS QUIET BUT IT IS AS IF SHE IS THE HOUSE, THE MEAL, THE FLOWERS, THE POETRY, THE GARDEN, THE CARDINALS, THE PERFUME, THE INTIMACY AND THE FRIENDSHIPS. SHE IS THE LIVING PERSONIFICATION OF A WAY OF BEING THAT IS TRANSMITTED TO EVERYONE IN THE ROOM AND TRANSFORMED INTO THAT SEPARATE PERSON'S ESSENCE IN A REAL AND PERMANENT WAY.

ANAIS: I feel like a troubador, waiting to know what you would like to hear. What part of **The Diary** would you like? This will be your last chance to ask me what's not in **The Diary**!. . . . I will read about a night - dedicated to women - the night when I decided I was going to write differently from men.

(Quoted from Anais' reading of pages 231-7 in Volume II of **The Diary**, *August 1937)...*

"Beautiful flow between Durrell, Henry, Nancy and me. It is while we talk together that I discover how we mutually nourish each other, stimulate each other. I discover my own strength as an artist, for Henry and Durrell often ally themselves against me. Henry's respect is also reawakened by Durrell's admiration for me. My feeling for woman's inarticulateness is reawakened by Nancy's stutterings and stumblings, and her loyalty to me as the one who does not betray woman but seeks to speak for her.

"They suddenly attacked my personal relation to all things, by personification of ideas. I defended myself by saying that relating was an act of life. To make history or psychology alive I personify it. Also everything depends on the nature of the personal relationship. My self is like the self of Proust. It is an instrument to connect life and the myth. I quoted Spengler, who said that all historical patterns are reproduced in individual man, entire historical evolutions are reproduced in one man in one lifetime. A man could experience, in a personal way, a Gothic, a Roman, or a Western period. Man is cheating when he sits for a whole evening talking about Lao-Tze, Goethe, Rousseau, Spengler. It would be closer to the truth if he said, instead of Lao-Tze, Henry—instead of Goethe, some poet we now know—instead of Rousseau, his contemporary equivalent. It would be more honest if Larry said that it is Larry who feels irritation because symbolical wine does not taste as good as plain wine.

"When they discussed the problem of my diary, all the art theories were involved. They talked about the geological changes undergone with time, and that it was the product of this change we called art. I asserted that such a process could take place instantly.

"Henry said: 'But that would upset all the art theories'.

"I said: 'I can give you an example. I can feel the potentialities of our talk tonight while it is happening as well as six months later. Look at the birth story. It varies very little in its polished form from the way I told it in the diary immediately after it happened. The new version was written three years later. Objectivity may bring a more rounded picture, but the absence of it, empathy, feeling with it, immersion in it, may bring some other kind of connection with it.!

"Henry asked: 'But then, why did you feel the need of rewriting it?'

" 'For a greater technical perfection. Not to re-create it.'

"Larry, who before had praised me for writing as a woman, for not breaking the umbilical connection, said: 'You must rewrite **Hamlet**.'

"Why should I, if that is not the kind of writing I wish to do.?'

"Larry said: 'You must make the leap outside of the womb, destroy your connections.'

" 'I know', I said, 'that this is an important talk, and that it will be at this moment that we each go different ways. Perhaps Henry and Larry will go the same way, but I will have to go another, the woman's way.'

. . ."All I know is that I am right, right for me. If today I can talk both woman's and man's language, if I can translate woman to man and man to woman, it is because I do not believe in man's objectivity. In all his ideas, systems, philosophies, arts come from a personal source he does not wish to admit. Henry and Larry are pretending to be impersonal.

. . ."As to all that nonsense Henry and Larry talked about, the necessity of 'I am God' in order to create (I suppose they mean 'I am God, I am not a woman'). Woman never had direct communication with God anyway, but only through man, the priest. She never created directly except through man, was never able to create as a woman. But what neither Larry nor Henry understands is that woman's creation far from being like man's must be exactly like her creation of children, that is it must come out of her own blood, englobed by her womb, nourished with her own milk. It must be a human creation, of flesh, it must be different from man's abstractions. As to this 'I am God', which makes creation an act of solitude and pride, this image of God alone making sky, earth, sea, it is this image which has confused woman. (Man too, because he thinks God did it all alone, and he thinks he did it all alone. And behind every achievement of man lies a woman, and I am sure God was helped too but never acknowledged it.)

"Woman does not forget she needs the fecundator, she does not forget that everything that is born of her is planted in her. If she forgets this she is lost. What will be marvelous to contemplate will not be her solitude but this image of woman being visited at night by man and the marvelous things she will give birth to in the morning.

God alone, creating, may be a beautiful spectacle. I don't know. Man's objectivity may be an imitation of this God so detached from us and human emotion. But a woman alone creating is not a beautiful spectacle. The woman was born mother, mistress, wife, sister, she was born to represent union, communion, communication, she was born to give birth to life, and not to insanity. It is man's separateness, his so-called objectivity, which has made him lose contact, and then his reason. Woman was born to *be* the connecting link between man and his human self. Between abstract ideas and the personal pattern which creates them. Man, to create, must become man.

"Woman has this life-role, but the woman artist has to fuse creation and life in her own way, or in her own womb if you prefer. She has to create something different from man. Man created a world cut off from nature. Woman has to create within the mystery, storms, terrors, the infernos of sex, the battle against abstractions and art. She has to sever herself from the myth man creates, from being created by him, she has to struggle with her own cycles, storms, terrors, which man does not understand. Woman wants to destroy aloneness, recover the original paradise. The art of woman must be born in the womb-cells of the mind. She must be the link between the synthetic products of man's mind and the elements.

"I do not delude myself as man does, that I create in proud isolation. I say we are bound, interdependent. Woman is not deluded. She must create without these proud delusions of man, without megalomania, without schizophrenia, without madness. She must create that unity which man first destroyed by his proud consciousness.

..."Man today is like a tree that is withering at the roots. And most women painted and wrote nothing but imitations of phalluses. The world was filled with phalluses, like totem poles, and no womb anywhere. I must go the opposite way from Proust who found eternal moments in creation. I must find them in life. My work must be the closest to the life flow. I must install myself inside of the seed, growth, mysteries. I must prove the possibility of instantaneous, immediate, spontaneous art. My art must be like a miracle. Before it goes through the conduits of the brain and becomes an abstraction, a fiction, a lie. It must be for woman, more like a personified ancient ritual, where every spiritual thought was made visible, enacted, represented.

"A sense of the infinite in the present, as the child has.

"Woman's role in creation should be parallel to her role in life. I don't mean the good earth. I mean the bad earth too, the demon, the instincts, the storms of nature. Tragedies, conflicts, mysteries are personal. Man fabricated a detachment which became fatal. Woman must not fabricate. She must descend into the real womb and expose its secrets and its labyrinths. She must describe it as the city of Fez, with its Arabian Nights gentleness, tranquillity and mystery. She must describe the voracious moods, the desires, the worlds contained in each cell of it. For the womb has dreams. It is not as simple as the good earth. I believe at times that man created art outof fear of exploring woman. I believe woman stuttered about herself out of fear of what she had to say. She covered herself with taboos and veils. Man invented a woman to suit his needs. He disposed of her by identifying her with nature and then paraded his contemptuous domination of nature. But woman is not nature only.

"She is the mermaid with her fish-tail dipped in the unconscious. Her creation will be to make articulate this obscure world which dominates man, which he denies being dominated by, but which asserts its domination in destructive proofs of its presence, madness.

"Note by Durrell: 'Anais is *unanswerable.* Completely unanswerable. I fold up and give in. What she says is biologically true from the very navel strings'."

Trew: I watch for Anais to falter but she never does.

Adele: All the times and hours I read from those *Diaries* and now the person who wrote them is reading and I am back again at that point outside the event, aware of the dream when it comes true - too intense a feeling for any words. A fourth dimensional event - time telescoped and expanded all at once.

Someone asks for a part from **Volume III** *about creation and guilt in woman. Written five years after the previous excerpt, there is a startling relationship between them.*

ANAIS: When I came back from Europe in 1940, I had a studio in the Village, and the custom in the Village was that people came in all day to your place. It wasn't like France where you wouldn't dare go to the artists, writers' studios, because in the first place you knew you would see them in the evening in the cafe, but also there was an understanding that nobody visited anybody during the day because you were working. So I found myself in the Village where everybody came to your place early in the morning or any time at all. I was swamped by young writers who needed care, who would help themselves in the icebox and take away my typewriter. I called it my cafeteria. Finally I got myself in so deeply that I had to go and see a young woman, named Martha Jaeger. We talked over this problem of my trying to mother the entire world.

(Taken from p. 240-1 in **Volume III**, *Winter 1942)*

". . . I abandoned myself to her care and felt less hurt and less confused. It was as if I had been given absolution and the permission to rest, relax, and give up my burdens. She was amazed at all I had taken on.

". . . she explained the urge that had driven me into this superhuman effort. 'Woman communicates with the cosmos, the cosmic, through the earth, through her maternal self. So you became the all-mother, giving out endlessly. You attempted to take care of everyone. You attempted the infinite with a finite human body.'

"Each time she mentions this I see the enormous loves growing immense and finally crushing me. And all this immense effort is reduced, simplified, and I stand naked and free of the giant task, a child again, relaxed and insouciant.

"This is a new drama. The father is absent from this drama. This one is the drama of the mother, of woman. I have been drawing closer to all women, lately, aware of their particular tragedy. I had been reading about the three stages of consciousness. Woman is only now becoming aware of her individuality. But also, as Jaeger said, of her different way of relating to the cosmos. It is a difficult, a deep problem for woman to commune with the cosmic. She can only achieve it by a universal motherhood or else the priestess-prostitute way.

"I crumbled because of the immensity of the burden. And the emotional substance I used for it, the psychic and emotional expenditure. For it is not only protection which obsessed me, but the giving of strength, spiritual and psychic nourishment. Jaeger made all this clear.

"It is strange how I turned to the woman and the mother for understanding. I have had all my relationships with men, of all kinds. Now my drama is that of the woman in relation to herself-her conflict between selfishness and individuality, and how to manifest the cosmic consciousness she feels.

"There are depths I have not yet entered, which I struggled to express when I argued against Henry and Durrell and wrote about woman in creation. I reread this tonight and only begin to understand it now because of what Jaeger said about the cosmic life of woman running underneath."

Anais is asked to read her farewell to Paris before she left in '39.

ANAIS: It was Paris at night, all black out. The war had begun in Europe and I was just about to leave and everybody was saying goodbye. We were so many foreigners and nationalities. When the war came to France, an announcement came requesting that whoever wasn't born in France to please leave because there were too many mouths to feed. The Consulate paid for the poor artists who couldn't afford trips home and sent everybody back to South America or wherever they belonged.

That's when I also had to leave.

(Taken from p.348-9 in Volume II, Sept. 1939)

". . . I knew I could not separate myself from the world's death, even though I was not one of those who brought it about. I had to make clear the relation of our individual dramas to the larger one, and our responsibility. I was never one with the world, yet I was to be destroyed with it. I always lived seeing beyond it. I was not in harmony with its explosions and collapse. I had, as an artist, another rhythm, another death, another renewal. That was it. I was not at one with the world, I was seeking to create one by other rules. And therefore how could I die in tune with it? I could only die in my own time, by my own evolutions. I did not belong to any epoch, for I had made my home in man's most active cells, the cells of his dreams. Through love, compassion, desire, you get entangled and confused. But the artist is not there to be at one with the world, she is there to transform it. (S)he cannot belong to it, for then (s)he would not achieve his/her task, which is to change. The struggle against destruction which I lived out in my intimate relationships had to be transposed and become of use to the whole world."

Anais also reads a section from **Volume I** *about Antonin Artaud and his interest in the theatre. There are pleas for more but Anais gratefully accedes to a respite in which we see the films of Ian Hugo.*

We view Hugo's film about his artistic progress from the medium of copper-engraving to film-making, called "Ian Hugo: Engraver and Film-maker", also "Bells of Atlantis" which is based on Nin's **House of Incest**, *and "Through the Magiscope," showing women reflected and refracted in sculptured glass and acrylic as part of an allegory.*

Trew: Hugo's films are way beyond the present moment. Such intelligent brilliance and such beautiful, steady hands. It is rare that the two go together so completely.

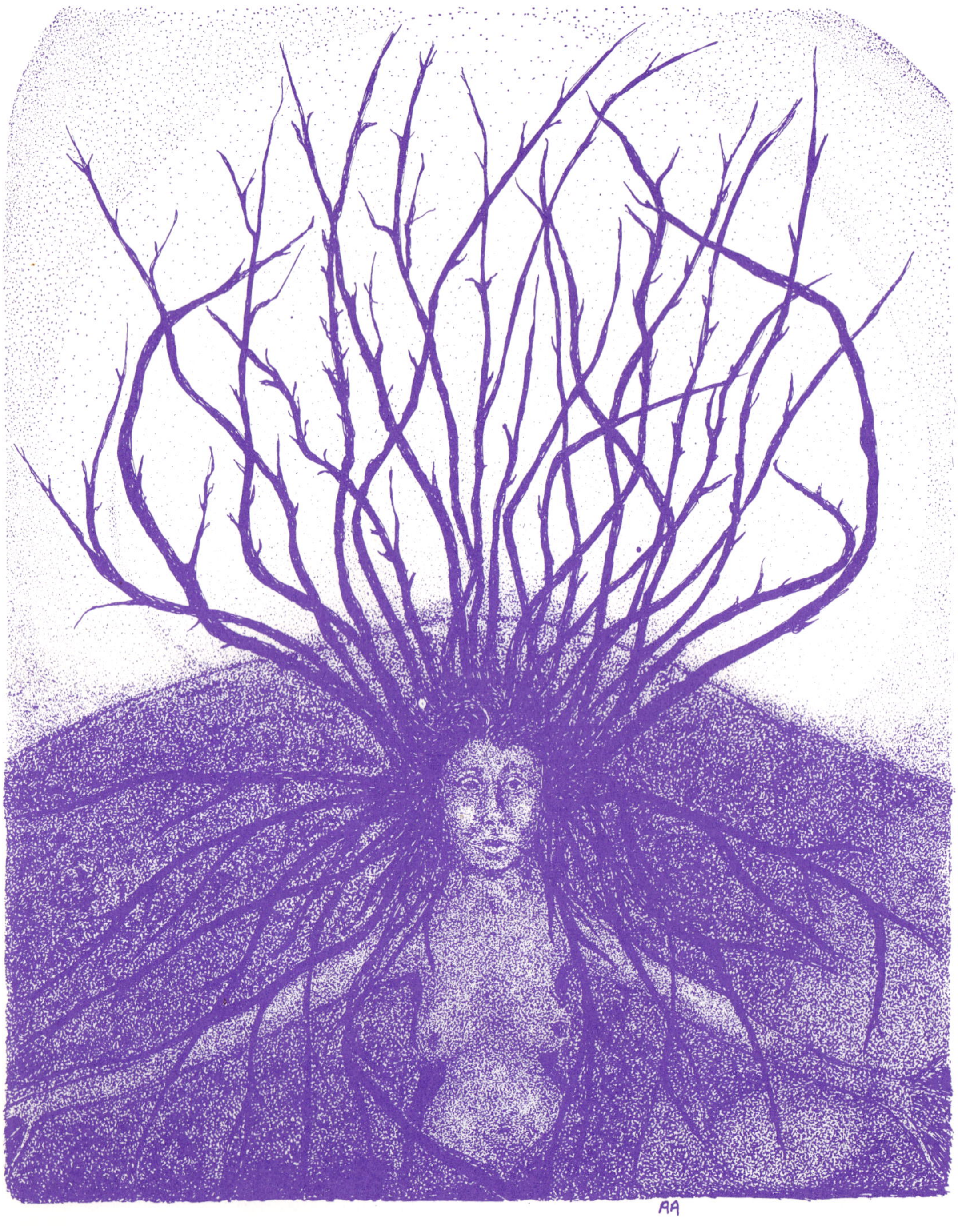
AA

One of the participants, David Williams, also shows us footage of a film, which he shot at the Pere Lachaise cemetry in Paris. Hauntingly, it contains a symbol of a woman standing behind a vertical slab with arms outstretched, which is similar to one used by Hugo in "Bells of Atlantis". Perhaps the image exemplifies how the mind's collective unconscious works, produced as it was by artists, working unknown to each other at different times, different places.

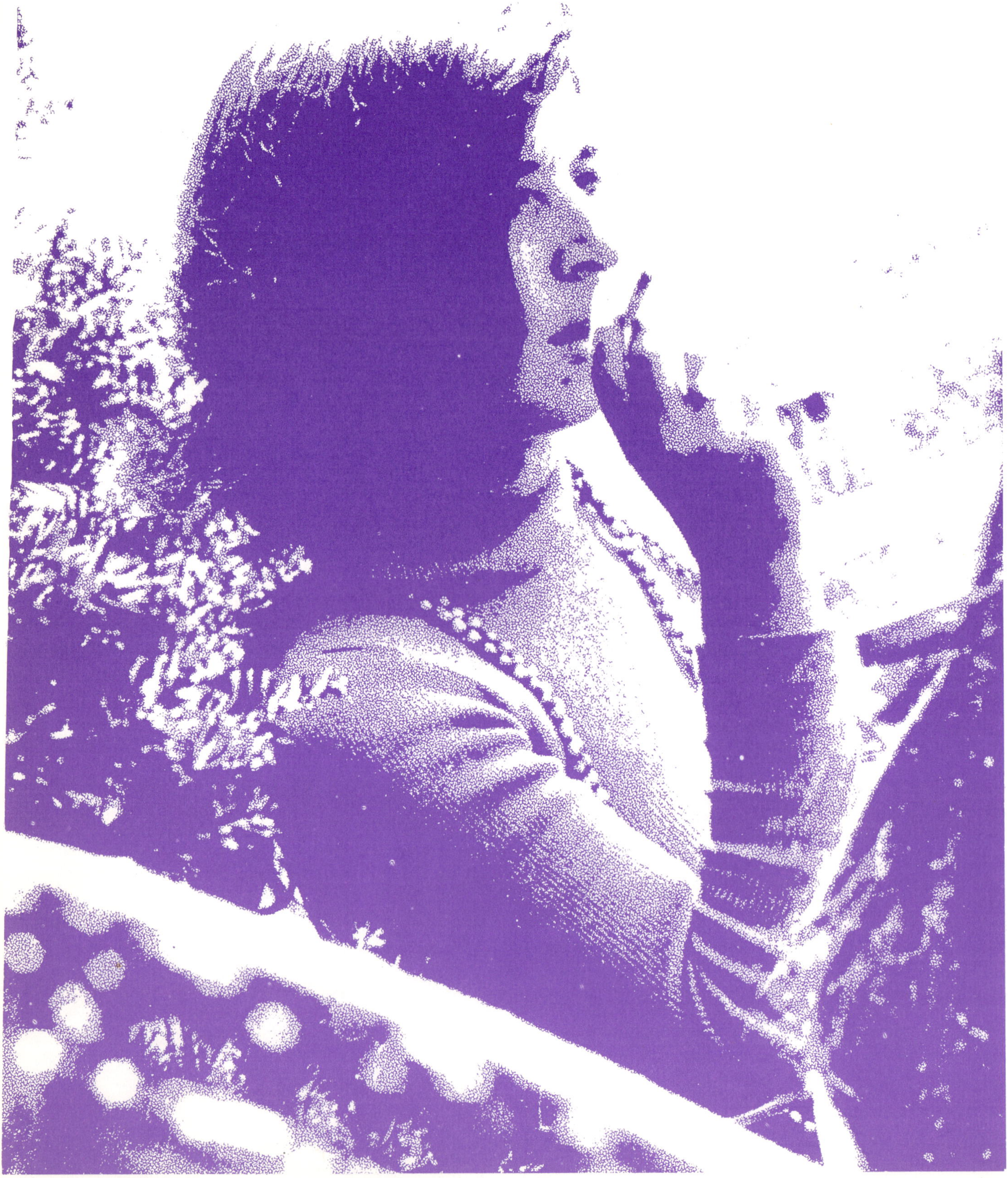

CHAPTER TEN

BEATRICE HARRIS: DIFFICULTIES OF BEING WOMAN AND ARTIST

To further explore Anais Nin's ideas, as expressed in her readings, we have a rap with Dr. Beatrice Harris, psychologist and teacher. The focus is on women, because the world at this time is witnessing the emergence of the independent woman, whose interior struggles and aspirations Anais has so well articulated. Also, most of the weekenders are women, a third actively involved in feminism, the others curious about the new "consciousness" of women. The men present are significantly soft-spoken, gentle, sensitive - and young. The group as a whole is concerned with the arts, many of whom have come to bask in Anais' sympathetic nurturance of the creative spirit in all aspects of life.

Beatrice Harris looks like she is both strong and independent, soft and sensuous, yet she remains elusive. She is young, handsome, with thick black hair hanging loosely over her shoulders. She wears a long tailored skirt with black boots. She speaks in a husky voice, casually puffing an occasional cigarette.

Here are portions from our discussion with her.

BEATRICE HARRIS: I have heard you women ask, "I feel so guilty... am I really free to create?"... The difficulties of being a woman and an artist lie in the struggle involved in taking the time needed to be an artist, especially for women who have children in our culture that has not yet involved men in child rearing.

Change has to occur in these areas. And the individual has to decide how she wants to take part in making change happen.

In our culture words like "feminine" connote dependency, passivity, emotional, irrational, love, roundness, softness; "Masculine" means intellect, power, aggressiveness, activity. Every human has these qualities but the difficulty is in integrating them because of the traditional connotations. Yes, there are differences between males and females but not to such extreme dimensions as has been thought. That is why people have difficulties when they try to develop an aspect of themselves, for example when women try to grow in a way traditionally associated with the masculine or men in a way associated with the feminine.

> *Ann Roche: Anais has written that when she first came to this country she felt that the women artists were imitating men, also that the European man was more accepting of the feminine side of his soul than the American.*

ANAIS: Yes, I found America a more male-dominated culture than the European where the conflict between men and women wasn't as great because the men accepted more feminine elements in themselves. We have to establish the right chemical proportions of these elements in ourselves. For instance, because women confused the word "activity" with being aggressive, they were afraid to be active. I hope that we can get rid of these extreme categories for men and women, which we have all had to live with until now.

BEATRICE: Because these attitudes are ingrained in our culture, we need to change practices outside ourselves, which means involving ourselves with the liberation of men as well. We have to learn how to collect the kind of money we need to have the freedom to create, how to raise children together and not be burdened with guilt. Guilt varies. In the upper class women hire help for their children, so they don't have guilt; in the lower classes there is no guilt because it is understood that the woman must go out and work; it is only in the middle class where guilt is a large concern. We have to separate what we WANT to do from what we SHOULD do, which is a difficult, painful, yet ultimately a creative process.

> Ann: Isn't 'nurturing' a quality that does not just belong to the maternal?

BEATRICE: Traditionally it has been the woman who protected the child from either too much or too little stimulation; who fed and allowed the emerging ego to develop, but it doesn't have to come from just one woman. In some cultures the man takes on the role of the nurturing figure. What the child needs is holding, warmth, being there, responsiveness. Nurturing means satisfying the child's needs, not developing dependency.

But nurturing is an important value in psychotherapy for adults as well. We try to develop in a person the capacity to love oneself and to give loving to others. Nurturance exists in and of itself and is not womanly in man but HUMANLY.

> *Lex Crocker:* Men have a harder time realizing their emotional selves because they do not discuss their feelings, as women do together.

> *Suzanne Benton:* But our perverse culture punishes women for this. When in desperation a woman makes herself vulnerable by expressing her feelings, she is denied and devalued. Part of the invisibility of women is that feelings do not count in the outside culture.

Larry Sheehan: One way for me to understand the other sex is in having a daughter. My capacity for putting up with change and feminism has been enlarged by my perception of what my daughter is like and can grow into. It seems a constructive way to look at change because a lot of men have daughters.

BEATRICE: Part of masculine and feminine divisiveness is that we try to separate our body and minds, to not listen to what they tell us. We cannot dichotomize the psyche from the body, because human emotions express themselves physiologically. There must be integration.

Larry: Don't you think there is an increase of people looking into their minds by writing down in journals and of organized programs for people to structure their own self development? These people seem to be trying more to get in touch with their feelings.

BEATRICE: It is a reaction against the mechanization of our culture.

> *Valerie:* This desire to be in touch with our inner core, this interest in the labyrinth of the mind and works that spring from the unconscious are the same as found in the period of Surrealism in Europe.

Anna Balakian: . . . because of the Vietnam War. We never felt the World Wars the traumatic way Europe did, but this war has brought us face to face with our own ghosts and disintegrating standards. In psychological terms Europe expressed the war crisis through Surrealism, which is happening here today. The results are the same because the causes are the same.

Daisy Aldan: At a certain point in time consciousness began to develop in man with a greater awareness of self. We are moving more and more toward the goal of individual freedom. It reflects itself in the Surrealist movement with the "Je suis" - who am I" - the question you see esoterically in the name of Jesus. Each of us in our diaries asks "who am I?" Then we move toward a growing consciousness, toward choice, and the capacity to change the environment. Anais always writes how change has to first come from the individual's recognizing and fostering the "Je suis" in the inner consciousness before one can move into the outside world.

BEATRICE: Not all people have the ability to reach heightened levels of consciousness, and it is the responsibility of those who do to teach the other people who are bogged down in currents of the daily world in order to produce the necessary changes.

I hear you say ''I am sick, obsessed'', as if your idealism and desire to create is no good, a negative experience. In the clinical sense OBSESSION means having no choice. Yes, there are difficulties in recognizing the choices we have, but we must learn to formulate new options for ourselves.

I hear so much diffuse anger. Justified, yes, but the kind a child uses to break free of home ties and assert his/her individuality. When the anger becomes focused it often is put onto the man without recognition that man has been trapped in the same perpetuation of roles as women have.

BEATRICE: Now, if a woman doesn't affirm herself, she is telling the man to respond to her in that way too. Women perpetuate this image to other women and to themselves as well. The important thing is to use anger to say, 'Yes' - Yes, I am going to change the system, because it doesn't have to be this way. Yes, there can be child care clinics and I am not going to feel guilty just because Nixon doesn't want them.

Remember that men are not free to entertain thoughts about whether to work or not. That is an option they cannot have. They are expected to be sexually masterful all the time, which is a form of oppression too.

Living involves us all in politics. But the ultimate goal of revolution is not to alienate men from women but the union of opposites. Ultimately how can woman create by herself, all alone? What can be created?

Georgiana Peacher: Man has always thought of himself as God, creating alone; yet women are taught to think of that as being destructive to themselves.

BEATRICE: We want human liberation. We want to emphasize our feelings and use our intellect to transform feelings into something. We know that men can be passive and dependent on women, that men can teach elementary school, that there are a variety of traits in either sex. We must ask if women are comfortable supporting men, and what kind of freedoms we can tolerate in each other. Sometimes when we haven't faced an aspect in ourselves, we reject it in others.

Consciousness has to be applied in all directions; otherwise it is like the lopsidedness that occurs on the pottery wheel when the clay is not centered.

Consciousness means asking not just why men are oppressing me, but how I am doing it to myself and how am I doing it to my children, and to men as brothers, lovers, husbands.

Shirley McConahay: Language labels our oppressions. Love is most expressed in competitive, financial terms by males and it is the victim-female who recognizes the put-downs the quickest. Our problem is to find verbal definitions for the complexities of our interpersonal relationships so that we can understand each other better.

Caroline Emmet: Everyone here has been referring to people as MANkind and using male pronouns when the sex should not be specified. We all are caught up in the oppressions of language.

Adele: I am sure men would mind very much if they were always referred to as 'she'.

Joan Anacreon: Our conditioning comes out in the funniest ways. Last night Elaine was showing me her sheaf of work. In it she had drawn a cow, which she referred to as 'he'! We need new words to express our humanity, communion, our oceanic feeling of togetherness.

Suzanne Benton: It is a matter of survival. Getting 'Ms.' accepted for women was a struggle and now even that is turned against you. The frustration for women is that we have to pay attention to those things, even when we know there are more important things to do.

BEATRICE: Yes, consciousness means recognizing the subtle abuses too. Recently I have resented the use of 'Ms.' I worked all my life to acquire my Ph. D. and now male colleagues call me 'Ms.', rather than 'Doctor'. But the question is where does one direct one's energy in order to be most effective in making changes occur?

Joan: Yet, we have the beautiful language that Anais Nin uses, which is so important. Each of us has to do what she can and not assume the whole burden rests on her shoulders.

Daisy Aldan: But with a sense of responsibility to humankind!

Trew writes in her journal: I have not needed sleep nor food here. I am existing on all these whirling energies. It is a very clean feeling!

90

CHAPTER ELEVEN

ANNA BALAKIAN: THE POETIC REALITY OF ANAIS NIN

It is our final formal gathering before the afternoon's offerings by the Weekend's participants. Professor Balakian is going to present us with a paper on Anais Nin's work with emphasis on the fiction, a paper which she prepared especially for this Weekend, and which subsequently appeared in the **Anais Nin Reader** *published by Swallow Press.*

Anna Balakian is professor of French and Comparative Literature at New York University. Her books include, **Literary Origins of Surrealism, Surrealism: Road to the Absolute; The Symbolist Movement: A Critical Appraisal:** *and* **Andre Breton: Magus of Surrealism.**

A colleague, Elaine Marks, professor of French Literature at the University of Massachusetts, author of books on Colette and Simone de Beauvoir, has been waiting all weekend for this moment. She and Anna Balakian, both having lived in France, speak French with one another, as well as with Anais.

In a private conversation with Anna Balakian she and I share impressions of France and the difficulties of raising children while following one's passion for literature and writing. In this she has succeeded so well that she is a model for women. She despairs to see good minds go to waste. We discuss how her sister, Nona Balakian, who writes distinctive book reviews for "The New York Times", is not given nearly as many opportunities as the men reviewers on the staff, which is a loss to readers.

ANNA BALAKIAN: This is a good time for me to tell how I came to know Anais Nin's work. As you may know, I had done my PhD dissertation on Surrealism and its origins and then I had gone on to teach Surrealism and written a couple of more books in the field. At one time I was teaching French poetry and we had reached the period of Surrealism - in those days you wouldn't dare give a whole course on Surrealism, you just gave two lectures or so - and Daisy Aldan, who was in the class, came up to me and said, "Do you know Anais Nin's work?"

I said, "No."

She said that I should because there was a relationship. And the next time she came to class she brought *House of Incest* and *Under a Glass Bell*. And that's how I got introduced to Anais Nin.

But the pressure of teaching kept me from reading the books until another student came along and wanted to do a dissertation on the experimental novel. She mentioned Virginia Woolf. And I said "Oh, I know of someone who is much more experimental than that - Anais Nin." I thought, 'Well, if she's going to be looking into Nin's work, I better know more about it myself.' So then Nin came within the range of my professional concern and I read her more fully as my student, Sharon Spencer, did, who eventually wrote the book on the novel called *Space, Time and Structure in the Modern Novel* in which she talks at length and very intelligently about Anais' books.

Then Nin's *Diaries* came and of course I read them and in fact reviewed two of them. In the meanwhile I got to know her as a person and that isn't always the happiest thing in terms of writing about a writer. In a very interesting article, Proust said that it isn't necessarily the people who know personally a writer who have the greatest insight into that writer. And he gave as an example Stendhal's friend, who just did not understand him. So it is a little difficult to talk about a person you know.

That's why instead of a casual talk I put between myself and you a formal paper. I am examining Nin's work this time from the point of view, not of the person I know, but of the text. I'm really giving you a structural analysis of her text and showing a certain evolution.

The Poetic Reality of Anais Nin

In terms of contemporary definitions of reality, dream, the human psyche and its communication through the mythology of signs and symbols, Anais Nin looms as a constellation of first magnitude. Since these elements have assumed greater priorities in the composition of the novel now than when she began to write, our receptivity to her work is more direct and propitious, than it was at the moment of the work's genesis.

Literary criticism does not occur in a vacuum; unless it is purely impressionistic, it can best speak of the unknown in its relation to the known, which means that Anais Nin's work appearing in the 1930's and 40's was immediately associated with the pattern of the successful novel of the time. But in *Cities of the Interior,* she was challenging both the realistic and the psychological novel so ably practiced at the time by the giants of American and European literature. To her, as she explains in the *Novel of the Future,* they contained a common element which equated them: they both over-simplified the human psyche and reduced it through rational analyses - too much lucidity, she says creates a desert.

But the desert of the European novel between the two world wars and even after that, was a fruitful one. Particularly as it developed among American writers who dominated the literary scene, it distinguished itself primarily in terms of three basic features: sociological realism, psychological rationalism, and the inception of demotic language into the literary context. On all three counts Anais Nin's writing proved unrelated to it. The great books of our era have from the point of view of sociology brought into crystallization the American mores, the strata of the multifaceted realities of such groups as the social elite, the ethnic separations, urban poverty, archetypal middle class heroes, regional deviations etc. When they have delved into the psychological factors that motivate the hero or antihero they have had a distinctly and rather superficially Freudian approach. The interior monologue, the autopsychoanalysis that predominated so many novels were indeed reductive devices that resolved problems in terms of a priori value structure such as sin, guilt, frustration, obsession, complex, elements suggesting the impoverishing or deteriorating qualities of the human personality. The built-in and recognized notion of reality presupposed a structure of norms; conflicts of the fictional reality were unfurled in terms of these so-called normal values, the notion of the tragic or the absurd resolution of the conflicts was dependent on the ingrained, collective determination of what is normal and what is abnormal, what is true and untrue, what is fidelity and adultery, what is innocence, and what is evil. The fictional archetypes either disintegrated in the process of confrontation with the code or they transcended it; but even rebellion was defined in terms of the concerted notion of conformity. Nothing is abnormal unless you first propose the dimensions of the normal; nothing is irrational unless you have consensus as to what is rational, nothing is unreal unless you agree on the tenets of the real. In a few moments we shall see how these significantly related to the life and work of Anais Nin.

The armor with which American realism covered itself was the development of a demotic language. Previously, even in realistic literature when all else was a transcription of vital statistics, the use of language created a distinct separation between journalistic communication and the language of literary test. Gradually the literary uniqueness of language disappeared and the gap between oral and written language closed, making this transfer one of the most characteristic features of our current literary form.

In the midst of this current toward absorbing the fictional world of the literary artists into the mainstream of phenomenal experience, literature in America gradually lost its ontological character: it was no longer a reality in itself but the written, documentary commentary of events.

Relating the work of Anais Nin to this literary orientation is like relating the plays of Yeats to the London stage of his time. If Yeats did not document the mores of his time, that was simply not the intention of his work. His was a poetic and universal reality. So is Anais Nin's. She does observe the mores and the places of their framework, but her observation is gauged on a level where time and region are not determinants of judgment and truth. Her work contains none of the dimensions of that reality defined by her generation of novelists: it reveals no group dynamics because Anais Nin's world is peopled by individuals; it contains no linear psychological consistency because in the revelations of human personality there are enigmas and half opened windows on their mysteries but no generalizations to guide us. If the rest of the world measured, mathematically speaking, according to base ten, her computations of reality had an entirely different base. She arrives at reality through inductive observation and experience of life; she projects the human psyche not through reductive, analytical procedures, but through a series of revelations, showing not deviations from a norm, but a fluidity of progression from one form to another. Her work has no trace of demotic speech. The language she uses belongs to no school or time or place, but it builds up its own code; words have their special meanings, and symbols which are culled from the common body of mythology take on particular significances in the code of her reality.

The first problem that comes up in discussing her work is the relationship of the diary to the creative writing. In the case of a diarist such as Andre Gide, the procedure is easy. The memoirs record facts, give outright confessions, which the critic studies to determine the creative transformation of materials into fictional reality. Knowledge of Gide in the journals furnishes clarity of comprehension of the man, and leads to the kind of method recommended by the 19th century patron of critics, Sainte-Beuve: to understand the work through the study of the man, for the relation of the work to the man is as the fruit to the tree. Following this precept it would indeed be nice and easy to suggest that Anais Nin is a fountain-head of sensibilities and perceptions overflowing into two parallel streams: one the diary, the other the continuous novel. It would be so convenient to propose that one stream represents reality, the other fiction. But the psyche of Anais

Nin does not project into written language in such a convenient manner. The diary has creative perspective, the creative writing is drenched in lived experience. In fact, the diary and the creative work are like two communicating vessels, and the division is an imaginary one; they feed each other constantly, the diary feeds the imagination with encounter and experience, the creative process invades the diary with its iridescence, transforming the perceptions of the author in regard to her sensory data and emotional reactions to events. Moreover, at times one has the feeling that the diary has literary structure as much and even more than the novel; if it reflects a life, it reveals, at least in the parts that have been published, *chosen moments, chosen events,* highlights rather than composites of personalities; the climate that the author breathes in the diary and that her characters breathe in the loose fitting pattern of the novels derive from the same perspective.

To grasp Anais Nin's notion of reality, therefore, I feel that it should be viewed as a composite of the two forms through which the author chose to express herself; and most important, it has to be considered in its evolutionary character, just as we discover that her characters don't reveal their truth in one portrait sitting, but as their picture is taken in successive stages as they travel from One City of the Interior to the Next.

If the work of Anais Nin is not compatible with the general guidelines of the novel, it is much more intimately related to two currents in European poetry and contains within its progression the special conflict of philosophy and style that occurred in the passage from Symbolism to Surrealism. Although Anais Nin chose to express herself through the forms of the diary and the novel, the quality of her communication and the pitch of her literary voice were much more in harmony with the poetic evolution of European poetry than with the American novel.

Certainly the heritage conveyed to her by her musician father was a symbolist one, that of the later symbolists of the turn of the century: Yeats, Oscar Wilde, Valery, T.S. Eliot, Debussy and Fauré in music, and in Impressionistic painting. Her early work is penetrated by many of the elements of a "Fin de siecle" philosophy and its delicacy of communication through suggestion rather than outright description. The large influence of music on human sensibilities, the rarefaction of the concrete, physical attributes of the exterior world, a language vague and evocative, emulating the non-conceptual communication which we generally associate with musical expression are pronounced characteristics of her writing.

The symbolist psyche was one of self-containment, introverted self-contemplation, preoccupation with inscapes; the symbolist eye sucked the material substance of the surrounding and turned it into idealized, formless, fluid images all bearing the imprint of the writer's own psyche. The language of the symbolist was a purification of all functional connotations; it created, as Mallarmé stated, the flower that is absent from all bouquets, i.e. the flower *as essence.*

As one reads Anais Nin's early writings which, as she says contain the seed of all my work, such as the pieces that constitute *House of Incest, Under A Glass Bell,* and parts of *Winter of Artifice,* the birth of the symbols that will eventually run throughout her work have their initial appearances: the glass, the mirror, the water imagery are images of the envelope. They cover, protect, separate, imprison.

The mirror is misty: vision like human breath blinding a mirror, she says. The atmosphere is pervaded with smoke, and low ceilings threaten us. At one point one is reminded of Baudelaire's imagery from *Spleen et Ideal,* when Anais Nin conveys the obsessive image of oppression in terms of a vast lead roof which covers the world like the lid of a soup pan. There is greyness in the air, and narrow horizons obstruct the heroine's vistas. She is at war with sun and light, hersmile is closed, her abodes remind one of Mallarmé's *Herodiade:* she inhabits cellars and belfries, she is as a princess in Byzantium - the mythological concept of Byzantium as a place of beauty and impending downfall, with which the symbolists identified their locus. The famous labyrinth symbol that will run through the entire work of Anais Nin is at first not a channel of liberation but the movement of non-voyage into constricted places, the refuge places where dream protects the sensitive creature from reality. To destroy reality. I will help you: it is I who will invent lies for you and with them we will traverse the world. But behind our lies I am dropping Ariadne's golden thread, for the greatest of all jobs is to be able to retrace one's lies, to return to the source and sleep one night a year washed of all superstructures.

The dream in this first stage of Anais Nin's work is not a source of illumination but a submergence. It is closely associated with the kind of love which is ingrown: that for father, sister, members of the same sex, all related to the cult of Narcissism, or self contemplation and self-love.

The route through which she moves is, as she calls it in the beginning: the route of the dream. But the dream has to be protected from the pervasive character of external reality. In this sense the first world of Anais Nin resembles that of symbolist heroines like Melisande, Herodiade, Deirdre: it is a distinct evasion of the brutality of exterior reality, effacing that reality to put in its place unrealisable loves, blurred, misty visions, subterranean tunnels constantly confronted by impasses, negative images of attritions and wastelands similar to T.S. Eliot's scenery in the first four lines of *The Waste Land* or of Stefan George's *Algabal:* garden of decapitated trees, dead meteors, dried semen, sceneries in which nature's power of metamorphoses and transmutation has failed. Even the image of the sea and the ship, which are in general liberating images, convey in the early work of Anais Nin just the opposite impact. The sea is associated with curtain, veil, blanket: My first vision of earth was water veiled. I am of the race of men and women who see all things through this curtain of the sea, she says at the beginning of *House of Incest.* The isle of non-reality and non-existence toward which she voyages is precisely the lost continent of Atlantis where the poetic vision of Anais Nin mingles with the lost sounds, lost colors, soundless music, and in a state where there is no cold, no heat and no hunger, and no weeping.

Fishes and flowers have the countenances and contours of unreality and artifice. Even in her use of present participles she creates an atmosphere of weightlessness reminiscent of Mallarmé's Coup de dés.

The first book, conceived under the sign of dissolution, transforms even the most common symbol of movement and displacement, the ship, into a shipwreck, a skeleton of a ship, choked in its own sails, sails which become ripped apart in a later image. The language spoken is the language of nerves: The shadow of death running after each word so that they wither before she has finished uttering them.

The mirror image is a purely Narcissist one in these early writings. It reflects the self-image and the self-love even in the guise of a brother, a sister, or a woman likeness. Our love of each other is like one long shadow kissing without hope or reality.

But if we have piled up the evidence to bring into focus the archetypal image of the Symbolist hero or heroine, we must adjust our lenses. The interesting word in the last quotation is without hope, **which in the act of desperation implies a desire for release and carries a built-in indictment of a condition. As in a musical composition, there is a point where the music turns, modulates from one key to another, so in the** House of Incest **there occurs a turning point, after which the ethereal beauty of the world of illusion carries an element of self-censure, brought to its climax in** Under a Glass Bell **and** Winter of Artifice. Without hope **becomes an anguished drive for self-demystification and liberation. The narrator and her alter ego, Jeanne, reach a position of confrontation and disparity. The narrator is led to the innermost haunts of the** House of Incest, **into a room without window, where the beat of time is lost and where everything takes on the static posture of finality; but the narrator refuses to accept the situation for the descriptions have a built-in vocabulary of criticism:**

The collision between their resemblances, shedding the odor of tamarisk and sand, of rotted shells and dying sea-weeds, their love like the ink of squids, a banquet of poisons.

Through the image of a modern Christ **who dreamed of having his skin peeled off so that he would be receptive to all the impacts of sensory reality, the wish is spoken:**

If only we could all escape from this house of incest, where we only love ourselves in the other, if only I could save you all from yourselves, said the modern Christ.

There are two other images in the closing sequences of the House of Incest **that prefigure the conversion: The tunnel that leads out of the house opens up into broad daylight. The other is an image of a dancer who dances away from those who are trapped in the House of Incest and gravitates toward daylight.** And she danced; she danced with the music and with the rhythm of earth's circles; she turned with the earth turning, like a disk, turning all faces to light and to darkness evenly, dancing towards daylight.

So it is on the word daylight **that the** *House of Incest* **ends, just as Rimbaud's** *Une Saison en Enfer,* **with which it has been compared, ends in dawn and with the rejection of night, and moves toward freedom.**

In the next volume the piece called *Under a Glass Bell* **is a portrait of Jeanne in which the narrator can take a more objective stance and cast an ironic look of censure. Jeanne speaks in a confessional tone; she walks into a house in which mirrors cover the walls and ceilings. The picture is striking and terrifying:**

Jeanne walked into the house and entered the room of mirrors. Ceilings of mirrors, floors of mirrors, windows of quicksilver opening on windows of quicksilver. The air was made of gelatine. Around her hair there was a saffron aureole and her skin was a sea shell, an egg shell. There was a lunar wax light on the rim of her shoulder. Woman imprisoned in the stillness of mirrors washed only by jellied colors...On her breast grew flowers of dust and no wind came from earth to disturb them.

The narrator's own confessional about her dream-trapped condition is manifest in the next piece called "The Labyrinth" in which the pages of the diary are likened to the labyrinth after she has given us several other images of labyrinth from nature's own pattern: soft turning canals of ears, honeycomb of ivory-white cells, leaf pattern of intricate flowers, network of streets like seashells. After the motif is established we proceed to the metaphor of the diary: Serpentines of walls without doorways, desires without issues. I was lost in in the labyrinth of my confessions, among the veiled faces of my acts unveiled only the diary. I heard the evening prayer, the cry of solitude recurring every night...The white orifice of the endless cave opened. On the rim of it stood a girl of eleven years old, carrying the diary in a little basket. **In her words it is interesting to note that, at the beginning the diary is a means of refuge, which, in retrospect, the author views with a certain degree of self-censure, manifest in words such as** lost, solitude, veil **and** mutilation. **Even as in the novels, the purpose of the diary as it reaches the level of publication will be changed from refuge to release, as Anais Nin reaches a change of posture.**

"The All-Seeing" seems to be a transitional piece. We are introduced to another labyrinthian character; but this time there is in him the resonance of reality even as the sound of the waves inside of a seashell. It is a story of the inadequacy of dream conceived as detachment from reality. And in this short piece we have premonitions of a new concept of the dream, it is the resolution of the dichotomy between dream and reality. The conciliation of the notion of opposites; Two people who love the dream above all else would soon vanish altogether. One of them must be on earth to hold the other down. And the pain of being held down by the earth that is what our love for others will be.

The narrator, described by Jean, seems like a prisoner about to be liberated, whose love of other prisoners is the only obstacle in the way of the open door.

Winter of Artifice is a crossroad. As the father image fades, the narrator gravitates toward the summer solstice. She realizes that the music of the father is still-life meditation. Music becomes rhythm, vibration, the spiral leading to reality. It is to be noted that if we compare the synchronization of the novels with the diary we find that at this time the author comes in contact with Jungian psychology, and in *Voices* we see psychiatry as a releasing agent. The dream's position is transformed. The Jungian device leaves its impact as the author accepts the motto: from the dream outward. Henceforth the images of descent into consciousness and dream, the spirals of downward movement are replaced by a ladder intentioned for climbing upward even if there is the danger of fire at the top. The censure of a total kind of introspection is more explicit: Bring me one who knows that the dream without exit, without explosion, without awakening, is the passageway to the world of the dead. *(Ladders,* p.151)

Now it is interesting to observe that although in the most fertile era of the surrealists Anais Nin was writing in a symbolist vein, the one surrealist she was closest to was Antonin Artaud, the very one who in terms of philosophy and physiognomy was the farthest removed from the surrealists. He could join the surrealist world only through laudanum. Pierre, as he is called in "Je suis le plus malade des surrealistes," is a creature who draws everything inward, a brother of Jeanne, and of Jean, and of all the other refugees from reality. His anguish had little to do with the visionary reality of the surrealists. There are allusions to several contacts with André Breton's cenacle in the diary, but they are not of an intimate nature. If Anais Nin identifies with surrealism in her evolution from dreaming inward to dreaming outward, and in her eventual philosophy of love as a dynamic release from the cult of self, of the luminosity of human character, and of so many other characteristics that can be identified with essential surrealism, it seems to me that it is not simply through direct influence that she reaches this luminosity and the identification of art as knowledge and revelation, but rather by being in contact with the same sources as the surrealists and by developing in the same direction as André Breton. The kind of psychoanalysis to which Anais Nin was introduced appears to be the same as that to which Breton was exposed at the Faculty of Medicine in Paris, based on the teachings of Pierre Janet. The distinction between Janet and Freud is precisely the distinction between psychiatry as applied in most modern novels, and the one manifest in Anais Nin's observation of real life and created personalities, and as it is defined in Breton's surrealist manifestoes: i.e. the exploration of the depth of consciousness as a power for release and domination of reality, and as a channel for the liberation of the imagination for everyman. The teachings of Janet had a tremendous influence on Breton: they showed him that the observation of the subconscious need not necessarily be motivated by the desire to correct deviations from the norm, as in pathological clinical cases: the study of the unconscious was meant better to comprehend the vistas of consciousness itself, to break the barriers of reality, to bring about a new grasp of sexuality, not in terms of neurosis but of its catalytic expansion of the sense of being and the comprehension of the metamorphoses of personality. In the *Seduc-*

tion of the Minotaur **the probe is likened to an archeological expedition** geological depths where lay hidden the imprisoned self. **(p.95)**

The art and life experience of Anais Nin are not derivative of Breton's but parallel, concurrent, synchronic. In trying to rejuvenate art by expanding the field of consciousness, they arrived at the same global definitions of love, liberty and poetry.

From the dream outward; **it is the same image that Breton gives in his** *Les Vases Communicants:* **the dream feeds reality and actualizes desire. This is the theme of all Breton's poems. To be a poet is to create this constant stream between the dream and what we experience when we are awake. Over this stream is the bridge by means of which the subjective world and the objective are in constant conjugation, indivisible. Soon, as Breton said there is no object, only subject. Lillian in the** *Seduction of the Minotaur* **associates her feeling with the Talmudic words:** We do not see things as they are, we see them as we are. (p. 124)

But the subjective vision no longer produces a hot house plant; it is projected into the outer world, there to combine with other beings, to make the inert objects unique.

The role of the novelist in this neosurrealist context becomes modified. The enigma of human personality is not resolved or reduced, but rather conveyed. There is no lucid comprehension at the end of a story but a synthesis of all the parts that have been viewed whether in quick succession or in collage, in juxtaposition or in superposition like the metaphors of a poem. The projected personality in the novel is a composite whole made up of the disparate entities that constitute a human psyche. When there is incomprehension between characters it is because they are clinging to one photograph of themselves or of each other instead of realizing the possible replacements. In explaining the alienation of Larry and Lillian in *Seduction of the Minotaur* **the narrator says:**

The passageway of their communication with each other had shrunk. They had singled out their first image of each other, to live forever, regardless of change or growth. They had set it upon their desks, and within their hearts, a photograph of Larry as he had first appeared behind the garden gate, mute and hungry, and a photograph of Lillian in distress because of her faith in herself had been killed by her parents. (p.102)

In *The Four ochambered Heart*, **Djuna's self-analysis leads to the same kind of realization:** The trap was the static pause in growth, the arrested self caught in its own web of obstinacy and obsession. (p.179)

"I is another" said Rimbaud, from whom the surrealists derived so many of their attitudes. In breaking the mirror that reflected constantly and hauntingly the single image, as we noticed in the early writings, Anais Nin lear-

ned from open contact with many others, from the richness of her associations, the variety implicit in the universal psyche. As we glide through her parade of recurring characters in and out of the *Diary* and in and out of the continuous novel, we may indeed be disappointed if we are looking for a totality of characterization. Totality means static completion. The characters of Anais Nin are in flux, in movement, in the process of becoming. They have, therefore, the flowing forms of Dali watches, or suggest power, rather than contour. One can indeed liken her characters to the word portrait that Breton gives of woman in *L'Union libre*. The relationship between characters no longer creates the effect of equating each other, dissolving each other, but rather enriching each other. This is how the relationship between Lillian and Sabina is explained in *Ladders to Fire:* They both wanted to exchange bodies, exchange faces. There was in both of them the dark strain of wanting to become the other, to deny what they were, to transcend their actual selves. (p.124)

What is the role that love plays in these later works? It is no longer self-adoration but a vitalizing force, projected toward the other and combining that quality that some have called "pity", but which may be better identified with "charity", caritas, in its etymological sense of total love, the generosity and gratuity of love, the semblance of the sacred communion. It is implicit in Breton's love poetry, in his relationship with his last wife, Elisa in *Arcane 17;* it is a running motif in the last two volumes of the Diary and in the last two volumes of the Diary and in *A Spy in the House of Love,* and already suggested in *Ladders to Fire:* Not to possess each other but to become each other, not to take but to imbibe, absorb, change themselves. (p. 125)

As the dream is projected into outer reality the notions of time and place undergo the same type of mutation as in surrealist writing. Chronology disappears because like Breton she is not about to give us an account of the empty moments of her life, or of the life of her characters. The critic Frank Kermode in his book *Sense of Ending* has well analyzed the mutation of the time factor in the experimental novel. He aptly distinguishes between the "kairos" of time, that is the dynamic moments that one can distinguish from the measured ones of *chronos*. It is always *kairos* in the *Diary* and in the novels of Anais Nin, unless she is showing the inertia of the other kind of time. There is, moreover, through the choice of highlighted events, an immediacy in the encounters of Anais Nin, whether in the *Diary* or in the novel, which make the present tense the dominant moment of action; in fact in contrast to Proust, who like the symbolists was an introspective artist, memory is cast aside by Anais Nin every time it interferes with the full enjoyment of the present time. Hers is a Bergsonian time duration, in which past, present, and future mingle selectively.

As for places, they are always illuminated in the later works, i.e. after her vision has emerged from the *House of Incest*. In some of Anais Nin's descriptions there is an emblematic persistence of the Chirico mystery of denuded streets, but as she pours the dream out into the familiar landmarks

in her environment whether in Paris or in New York it takes on the glow of adventure or an unexpectedly explosive vitality. She devoured the noises of the street . . . she was only the finger of a whole bigger body, a body hungry, thirsty, avid. *Ladders to Fire*, p.88)

The symbols of darkness, misty, cloudy skies disappear and are replaced by a search for luminosity just as in Breton's poetry. Breton once said that man's greatest curse was his opacity. A good part of Anais Nin's work is this journey from opacity to light. On the way she discovers phosphorescence, which becomes a dominant motif both in the *Diary* **and in the novels; in fact her attraction to people or the attraction of her characters to each other depends a great deal on the degree of phosphorescence that radiates from them. The albatross image in her work does not have the emblematic character of Baudelaire's albatross. In Baudelaire's poem the albatross represented the mighty poet, clumsy in ordinary life activities as he is brought down to earth, just as the mariners bring the mighty albatross down to their deck; Anais Nin is attracted to the albatross because it has a phosphorescent glow. She explains it beautifully in the fourth volume of the** *Diary* **in connection with her lack of rapport with Edmund Wilson:**

Wilson, if he ever tastes of me, will be eating a substance not good for him, some phosphorescent matter which illuminates the soul and does not answer to lust. Impossessible, for we are children of the albatross, and our luminosity is a poison!

All the way through her many encounters she searches for the children of the albatross, those humans, mostly young, who still preserve the luminous center of their essence. It is the sign of their inner dream: each one threw upon the spotlight of his inner dream, **she says in the** *Children of the Albatross.* **In** *Ladders to Fire* **she describes another character as having** eyes which left phosphorescent streaks.

As for the labyrinth, it occupies in Anais Nin's work as important a place as in that of many of contemporary writers such as Breton, Beckett, Alain Robbe-Grillet, Octavio Paz, Luis Borges, and others. To look at some of these others first, the same mythological emblem serves many purposes. In the symbolist frame of reference it signifies refuge and barrier, conveying the feeling of being trapped. In the nonanthropocentric world of Beckett and Alain Robbe-Grillet, it is the symbol of confusion and drifting. For Breton and for Octavio Paz it symbolizes man's conquest of obstacles in his effort toward liberation and the liberation of the spirit.

In Anais Nin's writing, the labyrinth is ambivalent and undergoes a change of function. It is representative of the human personality. At first it is constricted; it is an emblem of fear and frustration not only in terms of the human being's passage through it, but of his fear of what he will find at the end of it. In *Seduction of the Minotaur* **we find in the beginning that Lillian came to Golconda to flee from the labyrinth:**

There were tears in Lillian's eyes, for having made friends immediately not with a new, a beautiful, a drugging place, but with a man intent on penetrating the mysteries of the human labyrinth from which she was a fugitive. (p. 19)

But as in the case of Voltaire's Candide who visited Eldorado, she soon finds out that gold and bliss and serenity can become boring if they are a constant; at least that is the opinion of another visitor, Michael, who has stayed around Golconda for some time:

The gaiety and liveliness of Golconda hurts me, like too much light in your eyes.

Lillian takes up once more her battle with the labyrinth and at the end of the passages of darkness she is illuminated by the revelation of its true meaning. Her own image looms, suggesting in the moment of self-knowledge that indeed we have to fear only fear itself:

She had come face to face with it, the Minotaur resembled someone she knew. It was not a monster. It was a reflection upon a mirror, a masked woman, Lillian herself, the hidden masked part of herself unknown to her, who had ruled her acts. She extended her hand toward this tyrant who could no longer harm her. It lay upon the mirror of the plane's round portholes, travelling through the clouds, a fleeting face, her own, clear and definable only when darkness came.

At the beginning of *Seduction of the Minotaur* **the ship that we had seen earlier in a state of wreck and destruction is whole again but still incapable of movement.**

This incapacity is brilliantly conveyed in the metaphor of a ship trying to move through an inappropriate medium, i.e. land. It is the image of desperate dislocation:

Lillian's recurrent dream of a ship that could not reach the water, that sailed laboriously, pushed by her with great effort, through city streets, had determined her course toward the sea, as if she would give this ship, once and for all, its proper sea bed.

The obsessive image of the ship-dream recurs again a little later in even more gripping form:

The dream of a boat, sometimes large and sometimes small, but invariably caught in a waterless place, in a street, in the jungle, in the desert. When it was large it was in the city streets and the deck reached to the upper windows of the houses. She was in this boat and aware that it could not float unless it were pushed, so she would get down from it and seek to push it along so that it might move and the street was immense and she never accomplished her aim. Whether she pushed it along cobblestones or over asphalt, it moved very little, and no matter how much she strained she always felt she would never reach the sea. When the boat was small the pushing was less difficult; nevertheless she never reached the lake or river or the sea in which it could sail. Once the boat was stuck between rocks, another time on a mud bank.

It can be observed that whereas in earlier books the sea was a covering, a mist producing envelope, here it eventually becomes the emblem of liberation. The passage through Golconda becomes indeed a liberating experience for Lillian because finally the ship begins to move as it reaches the element through which it can function:

Today she was fully aware that the dream of pushing the boat through waterless streets was ended. In Golconda she had attained a flowing life, a flowing journey. It was not only the presence of water, but the natives' flowing rhythm: they never became caught in the past, or stagnated while waiting for the future. Like children, they lived completely in the present.

Actually the dream-ship splits into two, the one representing the heavy, static position of the persistence of memory; the other the floating one on the route to discovery. The ship is metamorphosed into a solar barque: magnetized by sun and water, gyrating and flowing, without strain or effort.

Finally, it must be noted that the notion of liberty in Breton as in Anais Nin is cast on a transcendental rather than social level. In the personal lives of both Breton and Nin one can observe a total absence of elitism. There is a spirit of comradeship, fraternity, and charity not of words but of deeds. Anais Nin's whole *Diary* is an eloquent evidence of this as were the works and conduct of Breton.

Although Breton had joined the French Communist Party in the early part of his life, for a few months, he quickly recoiled from the leveling process of the human spirit, which he observed in terms of that ideology. His notion of liberty had a personal basis. He thought that woman should assume a new role as a liberator and guardian of the free human spirit. His description of the ideal woman could well fit Anais Nin both in embodiment and purpose: "The crisis is so acute that I personally find no solution; the time must have come to make way for the ideas of woman, instead of those of man, whose failure is consummate today." *(Arcane 17)*

If there is a unifying motif in all that Anais Nin has written it is precisely the theme of liberation. All exercises in search whether inward or outward are motivated by the drive toward freedom; freedom from heritage, freedom from binding memories, freedom from growth-stunting inhibitions, freedom from ill-conceived unions.

If music is the initial ally of Anais Nin's writings, art replaces it little by little as the objective correlative. In *Seduction of the Minotaur* there is the emblem of a free and open canvas, with elements left out allowing each spectator the freedom to fill in the spaces for himself. The missing elements of the half-empty canvas were important because they were the only spaces in which human imagination could draw its own inferences, its own architecture from its private myths, its streets and personages from a private world. (p.61)

In a later volume, *Collages,* she talks mostly of painters: the woman artist, Renate, who has also a hobby of opening the cages of imprisoned animals, and Varda, he of the landscapes of joy who replaces the father image of the earlier works.

He was the alchemist searching only for what he could transmute into gold. It could have been a portrait of Andre Breton who in old age talked more and more about the philosopher's stone and focused his activities on the search for the magnetic and unifying elements of the universe.

The landscapes of Varda create a climate far removed from that of *House of Incest*. It is an atmosphere permeated with light, not light of the moon but of the sun:

In his landscapes of joy, women became staminated flowers, and flowers women. They were as fragrant as if he had painted them with thyme, saffron and curry. They were translucent and airy, carrying their Arabian Night's cities like nebulous scarves around their lucite necks.

Although earlier in her work Anais Nin had sought the quality of phosphorescence in the young, she found the most luminosity in the older Varda. Actually, Varda becomes the archetype of the artist whose language and visions transcend those of youth and those provoked in the non-artist by hallucinatory drugs like LSD. Varda has the power contained in all the words that begin with the prefix "trans:"

What I wanted to teach you is contained in one page of the dictionary. It is all the words beginning with trans: transfigure, transport, transcend, translucent, transgression, transform, transmit, transmute, transpire, and all the trans-Siberian voyages.

The parable that follows is the implementation of the motto we had noted earlier: from the dream outward. It is the simple story of a blind man whose only knowledge of reality came to him from the descriptions that his daughter made of it. When miraculously his blindness is cured, he discovers how far removed reality was from the image that his daughter had conveyed to him, But, says Anais Nin, he did not die of shock. Instead he told his daughter: It is true that the world you described does not exist but as you built that image so carefully in my mind and I can still see it so vividly, we can now set about to build it just as you made me see it.

So, the eventual impact of the work of Anais Nin is very close to that of Andre Breton: the search for luminosity through the cult and realization of the dream, through the effort to preserve the phosphorescent child image of ourselves, through the expanding consciousness that love in all its forms creates, through art which is a more sensitive instrument than a seismograph, recording the artist's passage from the mudbanks of sterile relationships to emergence into the regions of light.

If the myth of the labyrinth suggests the confusion of modern man's mind and his progression through human contacts and contingent event, identified in Anais Nin's work with the very human and vulnerable personality of the artist, the myth of the philosopher's stone, is identified here also with the image of the artist, but an artist who has become almost transhuman: the myth of the philosopher's stone becomes the victory over the labyrinth, the power of creation, inherent in the human context, but passively dormant in most people. The artist is she who can put the latent power into motion and transmit the power of seeing which is native but unexploited in most humans.

There is a marvelous juxtaposition possible between *Seduction of the Minotaur* and *Collages*.
 Seduction presents a landscape of gold, exterior to the viewer and which becomes monotonous and inert for those who merely pass through it. In *Collages* the golden landscapes are produced from within, and therefore their impact is dynamic and contagious. Golconda is metaphorically speaking the divinity of nature; in *Collages* we are confronted with the divinity of man. In the final pages of *Collages* Anais Nin's parable of the writer who meets the incarnation of one of his characters brings into focus the universal truth of the relationship essential between the outer world and the artist's inner one:

We are indispensable to each other. I to your work and you to my life. Without me spending your words you may not be incited to mint new ones. I am the spendthrift and you the coiner. We cannot live completely apart. (p.161)

We can conclude by saying that there is in the work of Anais Nin a progression and an evolution discernible in the changing patterns of her mythological motifs. If I traced the work's passage from the orbit of symbolism to that of surrealism, it does not mean that this is the only curb possible to draw in her multifaceted writings. As T.S. Eliot said: "You cannot value the artist alone; you must set him in contrast and comparison among the dead. I mean this as a principle of esthetic, not merely historical criticism."

The essential quality of her writing is that it possesses, like the best creative works of our time in all the branches of the arts, that magnetic quality which provokes in each serious viewer or reader the power to partake, to relate, to become, by breaking down the barrier between the artist and his public.

The applause for Anna Balakian's illumination of Nin's work is long and intense. Everyone is stunned by the brilliance of Balakian's wisdom and understanding. Anais herself wordlessly comes forward to embrace Anna. Truly a memorable moment.

Trew: Anna Balakian creates the most religious Sunday morning I have ever experienced. I get a feeling of great completeness from her. She enjoys an authority which she uses kindly. Deep and penetrating eyes — her mind looks directly at me with no veil.

Adele: One look at Anais embracing Anna and the tears streaming down Valerie's face and I have to leave the room, unable to contain my emotions.

CHAPTER TWELVE
PRESENTATIONS BY CELEBRANTS

We have our last meal together. People talk in clusters and are reluctant to part, aware that the end is near. Finally we assemble for an exhibition by participants of their own work.

I show my slides of women artists at work and read from the manuscript of my book, a chapter on "fears" in women.

And Jeffery Mundy shows slides of his "night" paintings.

Then we move out of the darkened interior to the warm, hazy sunlight. We sit on the lawn near the flowing waters of the Sound. Anais sits for a while on the grass with the others and then moves to a chair in the shade. All around us new buds burst forth and birds clamor in the trees; it is Spring. There is such a chaos of burgeoning nature and tumultuous emotions that it is hard sometimes to attend to what is being said.

Sas Colby floats over the lawn in a series of fantasy masks and capes that exalt the imagination, chanting, as bells tinkle:

The point, my friends, is to enjoy. I will take you to a feast of fools, and we will give ourselves to celebration...
but I am afraid to look into your faces and see you looking back to me...
You will see only what I want you to see...
Today I am a butterfly spreading my wings and searching for happiness...
When I find happiness I will search for more...
Now I am in a vast field of flowers with music, color, and joy...
I see a figure dressed in a long cape with a high collar framing her head...

The atmosphere entices people toward openness. Jeffery and James Mundy read to us from their book, called **Blueprints,** *which James is in the process of printing himself. Here is a broadsheet from their book, which they later dedicate to Magic Circles.*

when in public
poetry should take off its clothes
and wave to the nearest person in sight.
it should be seen in the company of
thieves & lovers & brothers
rather than that of journalists & publishers.
it should fall in love with children
and woo them with fairytales.
it should guide those ones who think they are safe
to the nearest busy road   and leave them there.
when the electricity fails, it should wear sunglasses
and pretend to be blind.
it should shout: EVIL EVIL
from the roofs of the world's stockexchanges
and whisper VIVE LA FRANCE through loudspeakers
on french flag day.
it should never weep until alone   and then
only if it has veiled all the mirrors
and filled all the cracks with powder.
it should wander in the darkness   until dawn
looking for rivers.
it should parade ladies in evening gowns
spotlighting white shoulders and painted eyes
and crown each man in tuxedo with drooping daisy chains.
it should rush emery boards to madmen   hanging onto ledges
                                                         by their fingernails

it is the last blade of grass
being picked from the city park.

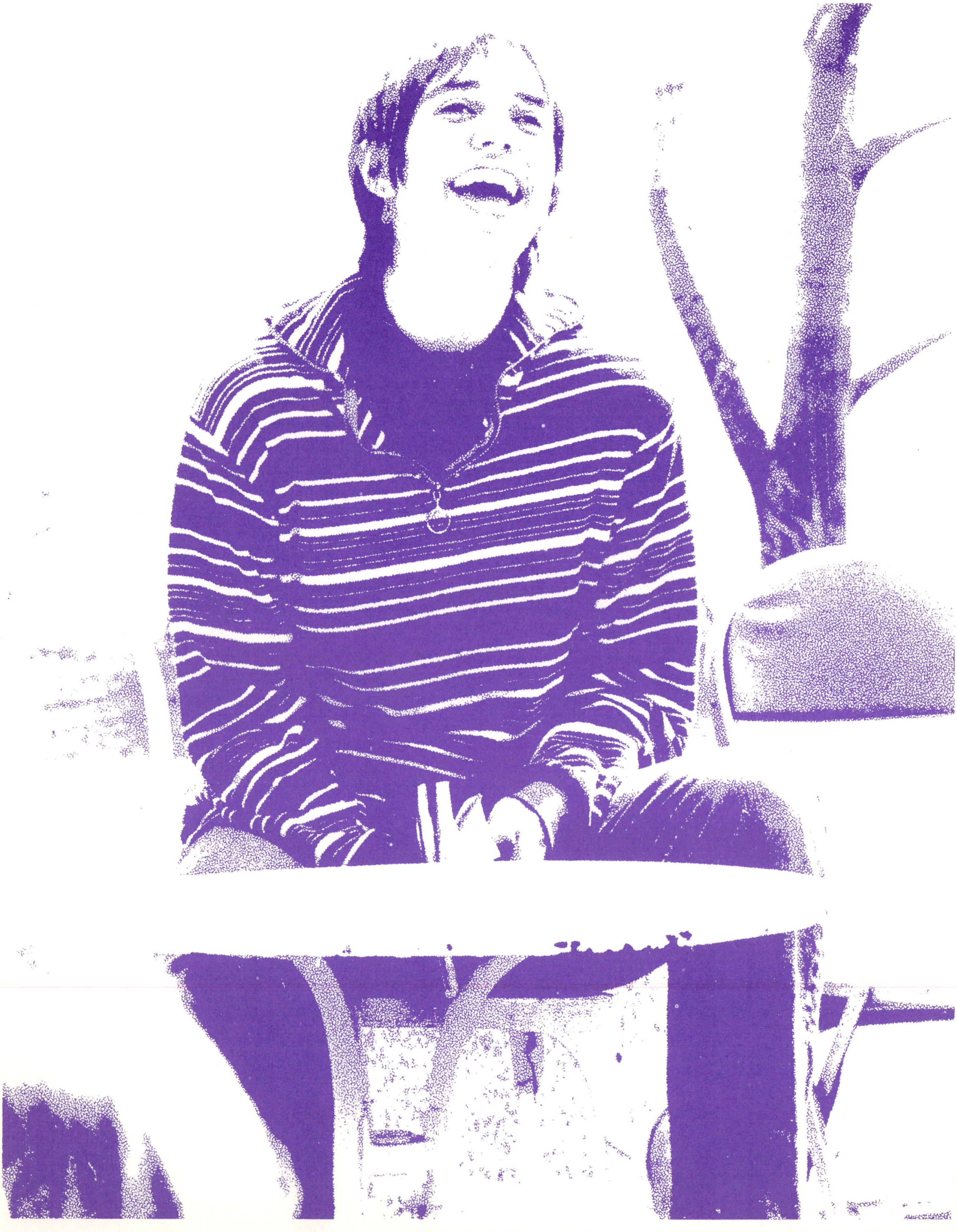

Daisy Aldan reads some of her poetry, casting a spell with her enchanting voice. These two poems she dedicated to the "women of the Weekend".

THESE WOMEN

On legs as sturdy as columns of marble
eyes focussed beyond banality,
they stride forward, wings in full sail;
their noble heads attuned to galaxies,
their soles listening to the heart of earth
pounding in primal hexameters.
As centaurs were half horse, half man,
these women are both goddess and temple.

OUT OF HER EXILE

Out of her exile
out of the blurred webs of her dream
out of the captive shroud of stony death
she emerges into a drift of light
which illuminates the flowering fruit trees,
their benevolent blossoms.

Star rays resonate
in revolving, reaching toward her
who molds herself forth to the encounter.
After long gestation in impotence,
she survives the major implorings, minor
retreats, dissonant defeats.

Weaving a cosmic
geometry in curves, spirals
and angles of the intoned Word, having
trusted its constancy among confusions,
one incredible morning, she raises,
stirs, chooses, becomes a world.

Moira, golden girl shimmering in the sunlight, reads a poem and dedicates it to Adele because it refers to the **I Ching.**

SEVEN EIGHT LAY THEM STRAIGHT

*THERE IS NO
WATER IN THE LAKE*
I cast
the **I Ching**
with pick up
sticks
over and
over I
ask the
endless
question.
Will it pass?
Will it pass?
This love?
This pain?
My marriage?
This day?

over and
over its
hexagrams
answer
in bright
dime-store
colors.
Let it go.
Let it go.
**SUPREME
GOOD
FORTUNE**

Trew Bennett speaks to us intimately about her relation to her pottery and says how:

My mother did not want to be touched nor touched me, which made me feel that if I worked with my hands, squeezing and making things that other people touch with their hands, that their hands would then touch me. More important than the pottery to me is the process going on, the circle of energy used and the cycles of creation. All of the body is intimately involved in kicking the wheel and working with clay, and as the wheel is going around, I go into the clay, which gives me a feeling of total integration. And I am very satisfied working with my mate. We each have our own areas within the whole and work very hard towards sustaining ourselves as potters.

"As usual" says Larry Sheehan, "I feel like **THE WEED IN THE GARDEN**", *and he reads from a comic novel on which he is working, called* **Luck.**

Evelyn Clark says, "I want you all to remember that revolutionary politics is based on the philosophy and logic of dialectics." She reads to us a passage from Trotsky on pre-revolutionary art.

Nancy Williamson reads from an essay called "I am——", which appeared in "The Second Wave:"

> I could tell you what I wish I were and what I've always wanted to be, but I can't tell you *who* I am. I could tell you what I do and what I want to do, but I can't tell you *what* I am... In the beginning my diaries read like this:
>
>> Today Margaret and I went skating. Margaret is moving to another town soon, and I will be very lonely.
>
> Now my journal reads like this:
>
>> I looked up tonight in the business meeting and Pat was sitting across from me... I have seen her almost daily, for many weeks, but tonight bathed in the glow of my strange new affection, she seemed a different person... I am in love with her, but I am afraid to write about it much less talk about it with anyone.
>
> ... At this time the journal is the only map I have.

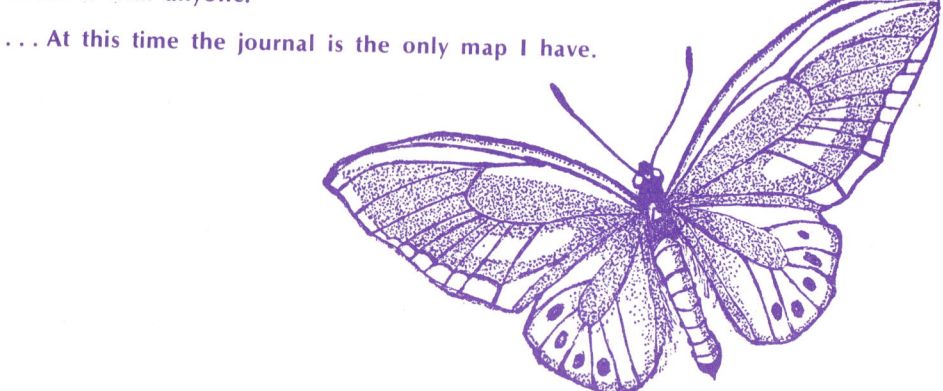

Shirley McConahay reads us one of her first stories.

Then Nadine Daily reads a chapter from her symphonic novel, feeling:

> Petrified by my first exposure... but I cannot think of any place I would rather be reading, even here my total being vibrates with each vocal cord, I embody every tone with its total emotion.

Suzanne Benton shows us her metal masks, saying:

When I learned to weld metal, I felt an enormous power at being able to bend, twist, separate, and blend the metal. It was like magic too, as I stood there all covered up in mask, apron, and heavy gloves, wielding the torch-flame: I wanted to create a form which would make people want to communicate with it. I found a theatrical way to use these masks in telling stories about "Women of Ancient Heritage".

In conclusion, William Claire reads several poems, one of which he says is about "proceeding from the dream outward" and is called,

LOOKING FOR A SONG*

The convoluted dream of the bug
going uphill through snow in poet's clothes
can rouse me from the luxury
of a Sunday morning bed and woman
to begin anew the architecture
of the lean poem aching for flesh
the narrative begging for sound
to strike the first note
the way a sculptor begins to chip
into solid rock long before
a form begins to emerge
the melodic pattern takes hold
an affirmation to live among the bugs
and the strange coherence of our dreams.

Kisses are given, tears shed. Larry, the magicians' assistant, pulls away the car to take Frances Steloff, Daisy Aldan, and Nadine Daily back to New York City. Everything becomes very quiet. Adele and I take a leftover bottle of champagne into the solarium, where watching the sun set, we talk over the happiness and sadness of all that transpired during the Weekend.

We feel fulfilled, for we had made our dream of the Weekend a reality for other people. The Weekend saw the coming together of bright sensitive people, the mystery of intuitive sharing and attaining new heights of understanding. Ordinary talk did not exist. It was an actual flowering and later we see that new flowers continue to open up from the stem of our dream.

Trew: The Celebration ends suddenly, as though no one wants to go through the ordeal of summing it up, or saying a formal goodbye. Everyone begins swirling up and down the stairs. I am aware of Anais, draped in a long scarf, still maintaining the still center of who she is, even at these teary and confused times. Adele and Valerie look at us as we scatter, like fragments of their dreams, before their eyes.

*Later this poem is included in a book **Strange Coherence of Our Dreams**, with poems by William Claire and art by Adele Aldridge. It is printed by James Mundy and published by the Magic Circle Press.*

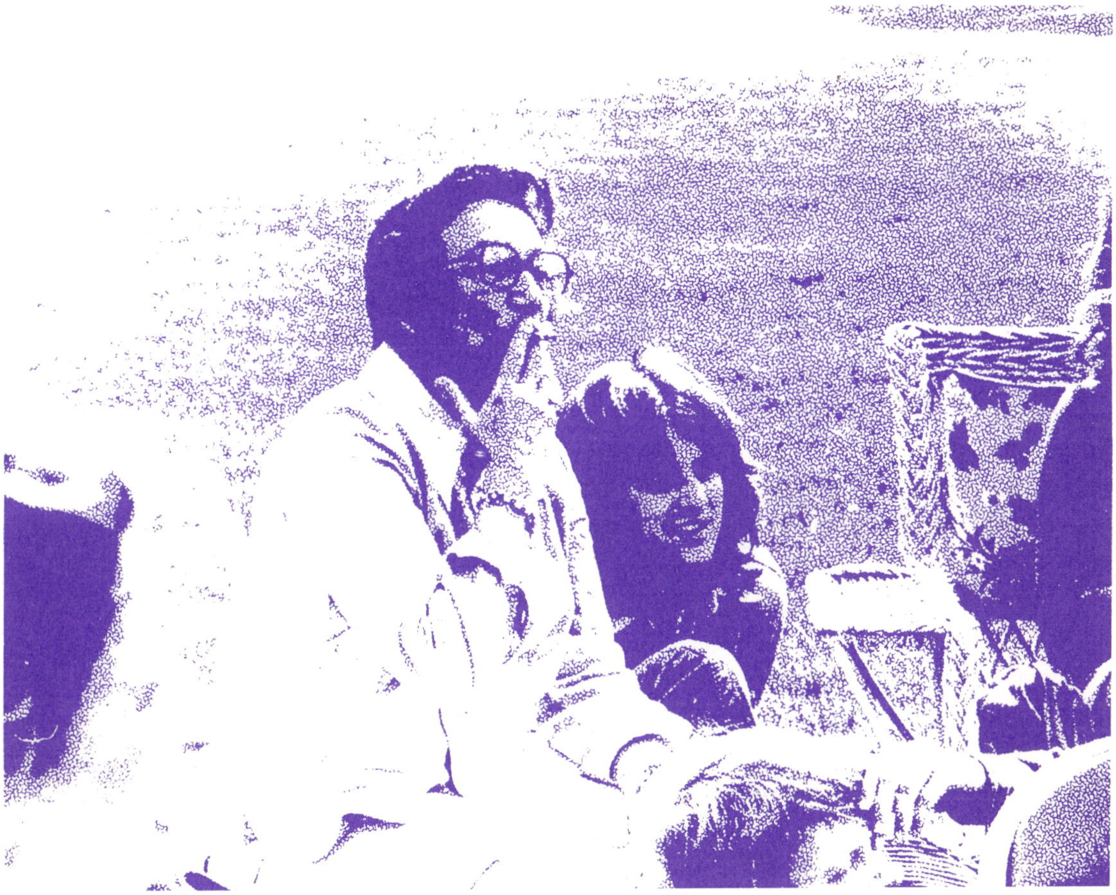

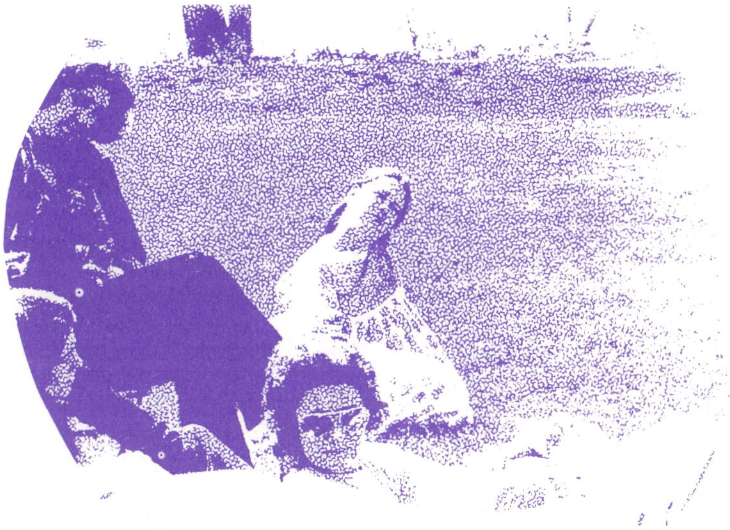

Part III:

Outward from the Dream

CHAPTER THIRTEEN

LETTERS AND THINGS

Afterward came letters and seeds of change. The words of these people reflect the feelings of countless others who come into contact with the transforming powers of Anais Nin.

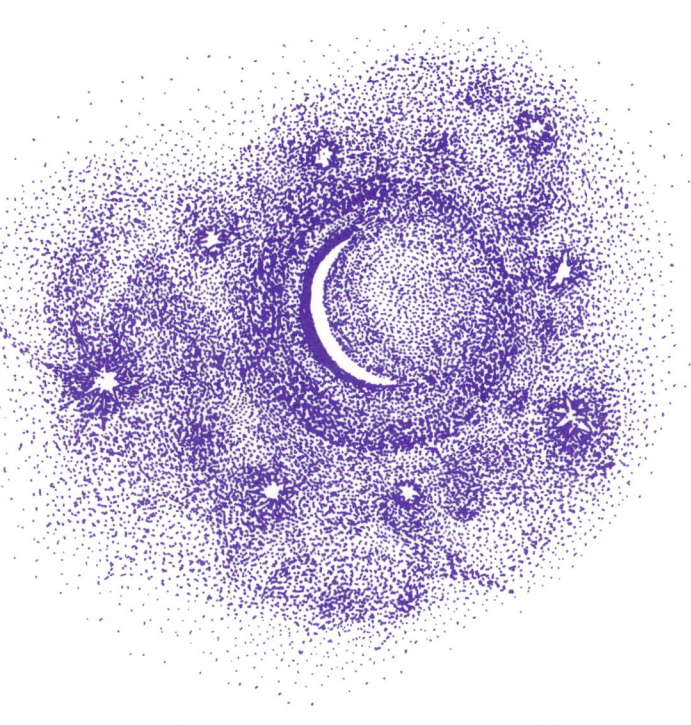

James Mundy: The weekend exists eternally for those who were there. It is focal and constantly expanding spherically. It is the stark beauty of forty whole parts (solid masses) coming together into a fluid. The atomic radiance of Anais in black and gold. The grand motherly grace of Frances Steloff with her long white hair trailing down her back; her robe. The deliberate precision of Evelyn Hinz, voice, her honest perceptions, mystical sphinx face. The deep velvet darkness, the sensual warmth of yes surging out from Beatrice Harris . . . (Valerie and Adele's) precision created one of the most beautiful movements thus far in my life.

Bebe Herring: The days in Rye with Anais, with all, were for me a birth. For years, I have been in labor with myself, and afraid to risk the final delivery. I think I was afraid of the responsibility an artist has, and I tried to escape it.

I have had a dream, always, of being in a "House of Mirrors", the kind I saw first as a child at the circus. I am standing in this dark house, and everywhere I turn, "I" am there, reflected in a thousand mirrors. To escape the House, to escape stasis, I must break the mirrors, one by one, with my own fists. But I am, always, afraid to raise my hand, afraid that one of those Bebe-faces is the real self, the real existence, and not a mirror.

Ann Roche: Anais Nin seemed a woman with a strong sense of her own identity and mystery capable of radiating hope and reassurance to these around her still adrift in a sea of self-search. She seemed to reach out her hand to me, as if saying step forward.

In Rye, I came to an understanding of my dream and an understanding of what I must do. I MUST begin to break those false selves, and begin right away. I have tried, for so long, to escape, to delegate my responsibility to others. "Here, you live for me." It won't work. So now, I have surfaced, come up from the depths of sleep, shed a marriage on the way, and I am moving into being through becoming.

Because of Anais' midwifery, miracles will be born of all of us. I have learned not to kick my way into the future or to hold, screaming, to the past. Anais truly taught me the importance of risking and giving. And we, all of us celebrants, have so much to give.

Suzanne Benton: I came home feeling as if I was a beautiful pitcher of white cream. The creamy contents had securely found its way to the opening and was coming out in an exquisitely sculptured thread.

Jeffery Mundy: The interstices are the places of the sources. When a hand is held, or grasps between grasses for earth, or reaches skyward; fingers lock, inbetweenness begins, and here, in this space of touching, the magic sparks are kindled . . .
the magic circles structure moved us into the desired state of mind. People there I am sure I love and know. If the artist is anybody, he is somebody to who things *made* matter very little, but who is obsessed by the making . . . the weekend is something still alive, it is present and still growing spherically. Ah, the magic of the circle.

Dr. Elaine Marks: Anais Nin is a most seductive and vulnerable woman. I made a great effort not to succumb; I was unsuccessful.

Helen Bidwell: Two types of impressions have been distilled finally: my shock at finding myself self-absorbed and stuttering about lack of content; and joy and calm and release evoked by memories of the events and people at the weekend. I thoroughly enjoyed the women, feeling very deep an affinity for myself as a woman . . . I am continually more grateful for the pivotal weekend handed us all.

Moira Collins: Anais Nin, by sharing her Way of Life has shown us that although existing can be tricky it still is a gift . . . My overwhelming impression of the Weekend was a party which never really started and never stopped, a continual celebration where one didn't have to wait around to open presence. It was a **VICTORY FOR BEING** party.

Lele Stephens: Two worlds, forever in flux, within and without, and only the artist, who dances on a silver cord between the two, can synthesize and illuminate.

We journeyed to Rye to meet a myth and found a woman. Anais Nin. Always and ever, in her art and in her life, inhaling the outer, exhaling the inner. We offered her a crown of adulation. She declined.

Something to believe in, *she said*, yes, that is necessary. But do not cast me as a goddess. I have come, like you, to celebrate art and friendship.

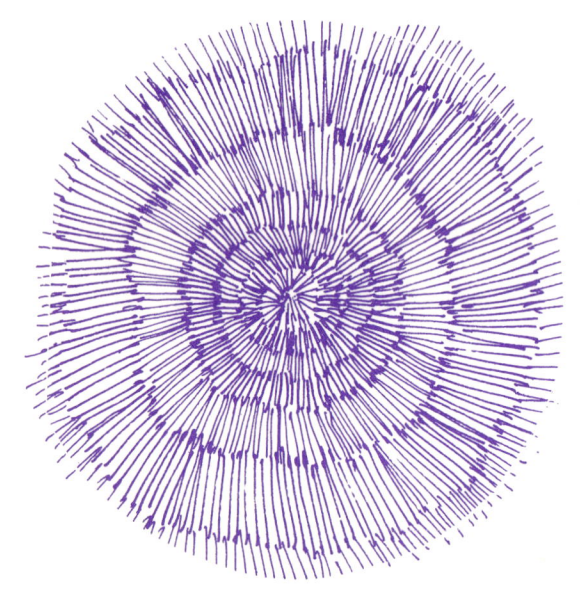

David Williams: It is pleasant to note the new emerging network of friendships. How quickly we got to the bottom of each other's natures but never to the usual amenities of age, occupation, and marital status . . . It became apparent that our most adventuresome and deepened encounter with Anais Nin would come through simple, more intimate conversation. She distilled in us all our normally scattered energies for eye-to-eye expression and listening. I'm trying now to listen to my friends creatively and with care . . . Also I now find my new allegiance to film is becoming more personal, cheaper, modest but fervent. Only in this way can one best approximate the self-expression that is usually, historically the province of the writer, composer, or painter. . . . The weekend inculcated in us Anais Nin's healthy creative, enriched approach to experience and relationship. A most successful transfusion!

Trew Bennett: The Celebration and the concentric magic circles are still in motion and our encounter is an on-going event . . . Anais inspired us to believe in ourselves as artists and to do it in our own way . . . My daily chores continue, my pottery spins, my friends come and go, and Anthony and I continue our marriage, but all these things are touched with the nourishment and awareness that the Celebration helped to create . . .
(about Anais) *She really is who she is* (echoes from *House of Incest:* Does anybody know who I am?)! She is all I fantasized and hoped she would be - gracious, warm, delicate, unique, and giving; I found her so whole. One quality particularly impressed me, and that is her seemingly infinite calm and openness juxtaposed with her gossamer aura of privacy, which never takes the form of hesitation, withdrawal, or "no", but is as elusive and beautiful as she is . . .

The Weekend fulfilled my desire to meet Anais and feel that there was exchange between us. It also brought me into focus with myself. It especially made me feel closer to all women *and* to the woman in myself.

Lex Crocker: I am still coasting on the energy of the weekend. I feel deeply that it has affected my life forever. My heartfelt thanks for awakening me to what I always felt life should be like, but which everything in my life and society had always negated. Those three days revealed to me again the possibilities in the dreams of childhood, dreams I had almost forgotten about.

Poem for Anais Nin

marina, gentle woman from the
sea
carries a book of dream-poems in her
hand
and sings under a tree to the sky
and the stars,
with a softness in her heart
and a tender breath of love
to the birds
which follow her
everywhere.

a tear falls from her cheek,
becoming a river,
on which people sail and dream
and gaze wondereyed at the
stars
never knowing the sorrow which flows beneath them

marina dons her golden wings and
flys away into the sky
leaving the birds to eat the
seeds of her fruit
as she becomes a maiden
of the sun
and spills her radiant rays
on you and me

William Claire: I remember the startling clarity in the eyes of Frances Steloff . . . the circular warmth of a library . . . a curtain string blowing in the light breeze . . . the shadows outside chasing away the doom . . .
what Thomas Merton called 'the hidden wholeness' in a country room . . .
Anna Balakian's mind bristling with delight . . .
Everyone tuned into the light . . .
And everywhere Anais moving like love . . .
with the grace and softness of an imperial dove.

Sas Colby: In colors the weekend was MAGENTA & YELLOW!

Georgiana Peacher: The world of tomorrow, creation and joy and relief from earth's avertible sorrows, currented in our week-end through live bodies revealing inner beauties on canvas cloth clay paper metal screen and waves of air placed in vibrations with interlacing tones from gentle larynges of sensitive souls.

I learned about prevention from work as clinical psychologist and speech pathologist, first in a veterans' hospital, 1946-48, treating men my age made aphasic and hemiplegic by brain wounds in World War Two, then at a university medical center, 1948-67, sharing rehabilitations with people from infancy through nineties. Undertowing every moment we thought that more could be done by prediction prophylaxis and that American medicine, American society circuited on base attempting cure after injury. In 1966 the oeuvre of Anais Nin produced a sudden and intense abreaction and rebirth in me, opening my psyche to new and immense dimensions of *life*.
In April 1967, I left a clinical professorship, headed for Paris to learn to live and write. I have far to go in this quest, but by my fifth rebirthday, as I began to fulfill deep wishes, comprehended a bit of my dilemma and ecstasy. For people who go mad, I sense they suffer from those infinite creations, innate in supraconscious of all, crying for life and also from lack of sharing, need for live interappreciation.

While we gathered in our island beyond time, my mother lay in a hospital, victim of a mugging, brain-damaged speechless and paralyzed. The reason I mention this permeation into my weekend is that this event would have shattered me with guilt and anxiety depression, kept me from appearing at any happy house had it happened prior to my freedom into creation. But because I've had time to write and think and use prior reception from year's affiliation with a progressive psychiatric department, I
 turned negative relationship into its complement, pleasure, by finally humanizing mythical perfection feels,
  met my tricky interior deviltrix,

   recognized my complicity with my forefathers "owning" men women children called slaves (dip in familial collective unconscious), my country's napalming Asiatic mortals and lands (descent in national collective unconscious),
    perceived my impotency as sole savioress of humanity;
     drowned beneath dissents to fish in thalamic core and there found the microscopically undetectable golden thread-link to exterior cortex-intelligence, trail toward controlled creatrixship;
      and thereby became capacitated to proceed without collapse into self-destruction as formerly occasioned at times like when a patient died of stroke on his way to see me.

   Celebration   Miracle   Furrawn
    inspiration of individuals
     bountiful variations in human gifts
      professional creativity in critique at
heights so delightfully free from pedantic violation to spirit.
       vibrant intrasensitivities sometimes subsonic yet electrically transmitting
portend to me a future explosion of these entities, helping ourselves and each other and continuing the apparent intensified efforts at heightened personal endeavors and warm positive relationships so evident in those who love the writing and essence of Anais Nin. This will live, this contagion, this ultraconscious. And to think, this culminated from work of magicians! Adele. Larry. Valerie.
I thank them and everyone
       which brings back the beginning of
        True US
         Not General George
          but Anais.

Beatrice Harris: Anais led me to the weekend . . . A flowing cape embracing her, she led me down the cavern that resounds with echoes of the past. Her words ignite a light in me, revealing wishes hidden in the shadows . . . as many times in rhythmic flow of words between us, she has led me to myself . . . a part untouched.

The *journey* is not unknown to her. Her eyes and ears unveil meaning in what others keep in darkness. I followed Anais into the house . . . It was difficult for me to speak the diamond meaning of Anais' friendship to the myriad of veiled faces in the room — my feelings felt too intimate to share . . . and all I said, too little . . . as one small wave is not the ocean.

I was immersed in and surrounded . . . by hands that created . . . that made beauty out of earth and cloth and color . . . that made paintings out of words . . . that transformed the inner world . . . by faces that spoke of pain and joy . . . and choices to be made . . o by eyes that delighted in their vision and some that closed out overwhelming light . . . by bodies that glided or moved assuredly . . . and others that stepped weighted with a burden.

Yet all were there to have fired the impetus to creation . . . to share with others courage and hidden dreams . . . and to seek in Anais the inspiration to walk a path, untraveled.

The weekend moved in magic tempo. First the slow building melody of voices bridging distance . . . the rapid beat when hearts have touched in common understanding . . . the climactic dance in words presenting inner revelations.

The knowledge burst . . . that I could too . . . that Will was conscious recognition of desires unfulfilled.

Sas Colby, creator of the fantasy masks and capes, is one whose life was to greatly benefit by the Weekend. She sells capes to many participants (including Anais Nin and Frances Steloff). Her work is well received in gallery shows in California, where she becomes friends with the photographer John Pearson, and on at least two occasions participates in artists' symposiums with Anais.

The weekend results in others taking dramatic steps. Adele and I, for instance, establish Magic Circle Press with the hope of reviving the love of books for their visual and tactile beauty, as well as for their literary or artistic content. We also sponsor another weekend with other artists and writers, many admirers of Anais Nin, based on Dream and Myth. Georgiana Peacher feels less alone as she works to complete the silk-screened folios of her novel. Trew Bennett and others feel renewed in their struggles to support themselves in work centered on their art.

Anais inspires independent creativity. A group of the women later put out a book of their own poetry, called **Moonseed.** *Suzanne Benton will organize a theatre performance in New York City called "Four Chosen Women", starring Anais. David Williams goes to Paris to study with film-makers, where he searches for a houseboat on the Seine. And so it goes, all kinds of new plants growing across the country . . .*

The following chapters in two different ways capture the essence of this energy.

CHAPTER FOURTEEN

I

The next day I said to Valerie
   what about Friday night?

we played back the first tape
to find out if it really happened

and the voices from Friday night were there again
some of them
honest and strong and disarming
some of them just fair
some of them just funny
some of them portraits in the Uffizi
some of them Canterbury Tales
some of them
lines cast to the center of the circle
just as we remembered

and I cried out

**WILL YOU MARRY ME OR RUN AWAY WITH ME OR SOMETHING
AND FILL MY LIFE WITH BALLOONS AND POPULAR SONGS
AND MAGIC CIRCLES AND BELLS AND ORANGE SMOKE?**

LARRY SHEEHAN:

I CELEBRATE THEREFORE I AM

II

The next day I went back to Wainwright House
to pick up pieces

    a display case in the solarium
    the poster of events upside down in the hall
    Sas' mannequin in a battlefield of fallen folding chairs

and Mr. Hewitt said

    WHERE DID YOU GET YOUR WONDERFUL PEOPLE?
I said
    THEY'RE NOT MINE I WISH THEY WERE.
    WELL WHO'S ARE THEY?
    I DON'T KNOW I DON'T KNOW THEY DON'T SEEM
    TO BELONG TO ANYBODY.

WELL ARE THEY ORPHANS OR WHAT?

YES THAT IS IT THEY ARE NAUFRAGES, THEY ARE ESCAPEES
FROM THE ANAIS NIN WESTERN WORLD ORPHANAGE,
SOMETHING LIKE THAT, FINGER-PAINTING OVER EACH
OTHER'S MESSAGES TO MAKE, GET THIS, IMPENETRABLE
PALIMPCESTS OF FEELING.
and Mr. Hewitt blinked and said
WELL THEY ARE WELCOME BACK ANY TIME.

I wrote down
    Power & Light Co. Nin
    Full moon cardinals
    Women in Love
    Yes

but later I thought
    WHY SHOULD I WRITE ALL THIS DOWN?

I am as surprised as Daisy was when her books
multiplied before her eyes on Saturday afternoon

now I remember helping to hawk the flyer
announcing
WOULD YOU LIKE TO SPEND
A WEEKEND WITH ANAIS NIN?
outside the Poetry Center
where Nin read the Artaud section and the Morocco section
from Volume I of her Diaries
on a warm night in January

my mission was simple:

keep flyers out of the hands of persons who had asked
foolish questions

I half thought
WOULD YOU LIKE TO SPEND
A WEEKEND WITH ANAIS NIN?
was a foolish question

but I did my job
and Valerie and Adele did theirs around the corner
and the foolish questioners did theirs
asking me
   WHAT'S THAT YOU'RE HOLDING?
and I would say
   FREE MASSAGE? WANT A FREE MASSAGE?
driving them off every time.

so there I was
someone who had not made the peace march organized by friends
from Amherst to Washington, D.C.
in 1960

someone who had not become too much of anything
for all that aloofness

there I was in the life stream, in life's dream as Valerie said
more or less political
at last

III

The next day I drove to White Plains
to return the rented tape recorder

and a policeman stopped me
for making a u-turn in Mamaroneck Avenue

I looked deep into his sunglasses and said
  **BUT A U-TURN YOU REALIZE IS HALF OF
  A MAGIC CIRCLE BLA BLA BLA**

and he said
    **TECHNICALLY MAGIC CIRCLES ARE ALSO FORBIDDEN
    AT THIS TIME OF DAY BUT I'LL LET YOU GO WHAT THE
HELL**

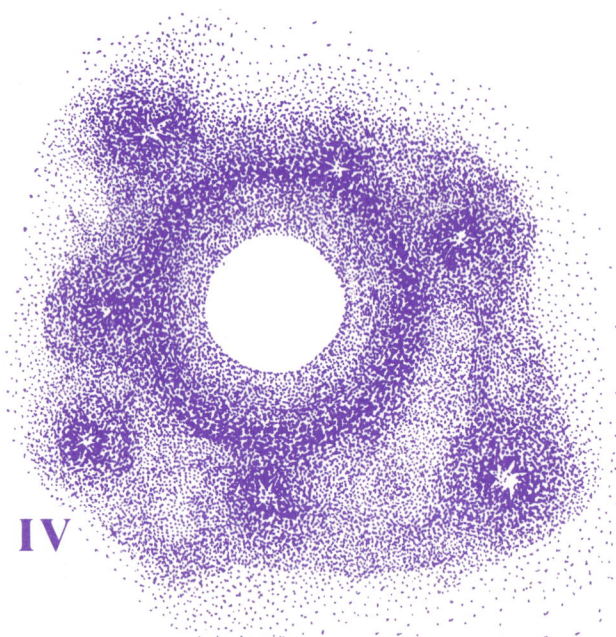

IV

The next day
Sas brought us bubbling Lambrusca and provolone and bread
and we had lunch together
and we kept saying
   what about the weekend
and
   what about the men, too
and
   what about Anais that Magic Circles Power & Light Co.
and
   what about the full moon and cardinals in the garden

and what about Georgiana
who came on a bus from her house on stilts
in New Jersey
before anyone knew room assignments
and I went up to say maybe she would have to move
when Adele's room assignments sheet finally arrived
and she said
    OH YOU CAN PUT ME ANYWHERE YOU WANT
and she kept smiling as if to say
    INCLUDING THE ROOF OR THE TOOL SHED

and two days later I said to Georgiana that was when
the magic started for me

what about those tall Mundy Bros.
upstarts from opposite coasts

casting lines about almost everywhere all weekend
crazy fishermen

presenting their poems
on Sunday afternoon
like a band concert

huddling with Anais Nin in the solarium
on confidential literary questions

what about how frightened I was
of Anais Nin

and Adele puts me next to her at dinner first thing and
there she was right before my eyes

and I have to say something ridiculous
so I ask to borrow some money
in the great tradition

and I tried to step from joke to joke in the conversation
  lest I fall in the lake
which is her manner of talking
and have to try to swim for it

and in spite of this she asks me questions
about my life and my writing

and I am eating furiously
including part of my napkin
and spilling Beaujolais on my legs
and passing the salt and pepper to myself
and back again

doing everything possible to keep myself
safely tucked away
and to ward off her jeweler's eye

but then I felt less frightened

and what about Evelyn Kleric
who is a revolutionary
inside a dancer
inside a keypunch operator

who said her purple robe for Saturday dinner
was the first dress she had worn in 2 1/2 years

who spoke and smiled with the radiance of
Consciousness VIII or IX I couldn't tell which

and read Trotsky to the artists
on Sunday afternoon

Anais: We need intimacy.

Evelyn:
I think what you said about the reasons you write diaries instead of novels is really true - that people really need the direct experience and need to unmask themselves.

Evelyn:
I was just going to say that when I read the diary I was overwhelmed by such a direct and honest statement; it doesn't have any of the constructions of literature. In many ways I was really looking for the diary. I was looking for that kind of openness.

and what about May
who came in like March
and went out like June
and who was easy to find because there were always
a few colored balloons in the air over her head
because of the nature of her wit

and what about Ann who gave me a book of hers and
edited the biographical copy of the jacket
before my eyes
adding scuba diving to her hobbies
and London and West Hampton to her residences
and three stepchildren to her family
and new books and stepbooks and husbands and inspirations

Ann and her friend May
those two smashing Manhattan success stories
with homes all over the globe and
thousands of dollars each
and better things to do with their time

like going to   than sitting around some
England   so-called Magic Circle
in the Spring   with dormitory living
                                              besides oh gawd

and they end up wanting to throw
mad formal dinners
and write about the weekend for the Associated Press

and at the end I kissed Ann on her
sunglasses
and May on her mole

and what about Elaine
who turns out to be May's niece

the place was crawling with coincidences
because of the full moon

Elaine wrote a book about Colette
and instructed me in some differences
between Colette and Anais Nin

and walked like a cat after lunch
all weekend
and got into remarkable yoga positions
on the lawn
causing various sailboat accidents

and what about Moira from Chicago

it was Frances who gave her
a folder telling about the Magic Circles weekend
when Moira was in New York
visiting Frances' Gotham Book Mart
where crazy fishermen shop

Moira threw the folder into the hotel wastebasket
and on the third day it rose again
and went to Chicago
and when Moira returned home it was in her mailbox

so she came

and when the definition of Commonplace Book
fell from Moira's lips
   what beautiful lips anyway
I finally knew what to call my growing collection of
Urban Mantra & Bumper Stickers

so I am grateful to that Magic Circular
that Frances gave out.

what about that fabulous vegetarian Frances Steloff

who was at the Poetry Center in January
when I helped distribute Magic Circulars
and at the Fifth Avenue Hotel in December
when I learned to keep the Intensive Journal

who let her hair down for Sunday lunch
   it hung in a pony tail
   between her shoulder blades
   gray as the mane on a wave of the sea

on the way to Wainwright House
with her six shopping bags of books for sale
and her sore right knee from falling
on the sidewalk a week before,
she kept saying to Daisy
   WHAT WILL I TALK ABOUT WHAT CAN I SAY
   WHAT DO I KNOW THAT COULD POSSIBLY INTEREST ANYONE
and **LUCKILY ANAIS WILL BE THERE**
and **LUCKILY ANAIS WILL GET ME THROUGH IT**

and she kept talking like that
all the way to Wainwright House

and then on Saturday morning
without a notion of what she did,
and holding three or four dandelions
in her right hand like a glass of water,
she opened her life for us like a peach
and just gave it to us

on the way back to Manhattan
she said out of the blue
   I BET PUTSY WILL BE HAPPY TO SEE ME
and I said
   PUTSY THAT MUST BE YOUR CAT
and she said
   YES

and I almost drove off the road, realizing she had been
daydreaming all this time about her cat
this founder of the Gotham Book Mart
this lover of living things
this uncluttered mind and heart
   who really can judge a book by its cover
this Penelope of patience and hard work
this lesson
this fabulous vegetarian
this optimist

in the car astrologer Nadine said
   FRANCES DO YOU MIND TELLING ME YOUR BIRTH DATE?
and Frances said
   NO I DON'T MIND DECEMBER 31, 1887 TWO O'CLOCK IN THE MORNING

Larry: *"What is Love?"*

Colette: *"A lock within a lock."*

Larry: *"That's a phony answer."*

Colette: *"You must learn to accept the sophistication of change. Love is a mystery. It is a lock within a lock. And the inner lock has still another lock within it, still more precious and tantalizingly secure-looking."*

what about those guest speakers
William F. Claire and Evelyn
going to visit the local cemetery
Sunday morning
when everyone else was buried in sleep

what an awesome thing to do

and in the evening we saw David Williams's film
about the cemetery in Paris
and he turned the graveyard into a city with his eye

and to top it off
Elaine turned around and told me
she is a stroller in cemeteries too
and that the cemetery in David Williams's film
is where they put Colette

and I remember Colette writing about
hearing her coursers draw near
and how that passage helped me set the scene
for my dialogue with Colette
when I was learning to keep a psychological notebook
and how that dialogue with Colette on love
helped me through the winter with Valerie
and paved the way for me to be in
magic circles
instead of vicious ones

what about the absence of keys and locks
generally
and that swinging gate near the water
that opened onto bramble and rough
  uncharted notions
which I closed for some reason
on a walk with May & Elaine

and then returned to leave open again

what about settling
the question of personal pronouns
at the oval table on the porch

there was Adele and Bebe who at age 20
taught Anais Nin the word **FURRAWN**
and we decided

HE and SHE may be sexist but
I is not and neither is YOU and
I and YOU
are the important ones
and who cares about
HIM and HER anyway

and what about Anna
with all kinds of degrees
and books
and a strong voice that made the tape recorder needle go
ZANG

she gave us words to use
like in-scape
and de-education

when she lost her car keys at the end
I saw her transform her purse into
a geyser at Yellowstone National Park

what a fountain of pencils and lighters and
credit cards and wallets and tickets to the theater
and degrees and books and new words and lecture halls

and then that psychic moon-fed person Daisy
and Mr. Hewitt who in 17 years
in the spiritual-meditational-philosophical business
has seen a lot of keys
come and go

found Anna's keys in her car

and she was spirited and brilliant again

```
          and what about            daisy
                                      i
                                      i
                                    i
                                  i
          as      POET
                     and as
TEACHER                    as
                               BI*Y*LIST
          S Y N T H E S I Z E R
                           and
   HIBERNAIAN                    GLACIER CRITIC
      JEWISH         &              FOR THE
   PUBLISHING                      NEW YORK
     COMPANY                         TIMES
```

I skinned my shin
on the bicycle in her living room
when I met her Friday
and then,
lugging down a leaden bag,
I wondered if there was a Singer sewing machine inside
or 12 pairs of shoes or cobblestones from Dornach
or what

but on Saturday afternoon she opened the bag for us
and out streamed books
dozens it seemed
like white rabbits

beautiful and apparently important
like a traffic accident on the table
right before our eyes

she said she couldn't believe it
she could not believe she had produced all those books
mostly for other poets and writers and artists
and not for herself
it was like she suddenly remembered
an old savings account

and once in her talk she said
    A FEW DAYS AGO ONE OF YOU SAID...
as though we all had been at Wainwright House for weeks

and everyone clapped

and what about Anais covering her face when
that line came back to visit her
   If Edmund Wilson should ever taste of me...

> There is no progress of the personality like a pyramid converging to a point of perfection. Fulfillment is the completion of a circle. All aspects of the selves have to be lived out, like the twelve houses of the zodiac.
>
> Psychologically, a great personality is a circle touching something at every point. A circle with a core. A process of nature, growth, not the ideal. The ideal is an error. Life is a full circle, widening until it joins the circle motions of the infinite. *Anais Nin*

what about Trew
someone who had made herself strong somehow

a potter living in Virginia
who brought color slides and samples
and even a brochure
but on Sunday afternoon
when she stood up to make a presentation
she did not need any of that
the work was incarnate in the person
her hands traced bowls in the air
right before our eyes

I saw her in the wheel while she talked
in the wet clay
in her firm oven walls in Vienna, Virginia
her life and work
   two horses in double harness

and I saw her in the vase among her samples
the one with a hole ripped in its side
for the form to breathe
for the evil spirits to escape
the well-gashed urn

I showed her my Intensive Journal
because it is like a hole in the vase
it helps ventilate the human spirit
it helps illusions to escape

and also because her eyes reminded me of my sister
who is going through a hard time now

she wrote down in her notebook
STEPPING STONES TRANSPLANT   LARRY SHEEHAN

it was like being published by Random House
what a weekend

what about when we gathered
with our bags and books and capes and magic
in the central hall of Wainwright House
at the very end

We were in a train station instead of
in the central hall of some non-profit mansion
and instead of leaving for South Carolina and
Wisconsin and Chicago and Indiana and Massachusetts
and California and Ohio and D.C. and Virginia

it seemed as if we were all leaving for Paris

what about coming back from Manhattan Sunday night
driving like crazy
to meet Valerie and Adele at the restaurant
and looking for flower stands along the way
I wanted to dump daffodils all over them

dance with those crazy caped creatures

and finally I find them
just arriving themselves

they are walking like helicopters
not gracious hostesses as everyone called them
and talking in champagne not English
and we go in and have laughter and tears for dinner
instead of lamb chops
and celebrate all our new friends

and I celebrate them
my heart is an open cafe
and I want to celebrate them over and over

V

the next day
we began to leave the in-scape

or did we?

my mantra is still
seven bushes spreading roots

my political affiliation is still
work and mirth

my habit forming drug is still
writing things down

the map of Venice is my unconscious mind
streams of pavement
alleys of fear
avenues of sea
churches of unwarranted faith
monuments of bad ideas
flower stands of love

I have a son, daughter, dog, cat and I
have not forgotten my army serial number yet

but the next day I figured

MY LIFE IS ALWAYS BEGINNING

VI

The next day I drove children home from school
and a boy said
   THEY DISCOVERED A NEW PLANET.
and I said
   WHAT WHAT WHO WHAT WHEN WAS IT OVER THE WEEKEND?
and he said
YES
and I said
YOU SEE IT WAS A FULL MOON AND I WAS AT WAINWRIGHT HOUSE AND I HAVEN'T SEEN THE PAPERS.
and he said
   IT IS THE BIGGEST ONE OF ALL IT IS EVEN PAST PLUTO I AM GOING TO DO A REPORT ON IT FOR SCIENCEAND IT WOULD TAKE 3 BILLION YEARS TO GET THERE.
and I said
   OH NOW I KNOW THE ONE YOU'RE TALKING ABOUT WE WERE ALL THERE ANAIS AND ADELE AND VALERIE AND THE MUNDY BROS. AND LEX CROCKER WHO IS THE TELEGRAM FROM TEXAS.

and I said a little later
   YES OF COURSE I REMEMBER NOW I KNOW THAT PLANET.

CHAPTER FIFTEEN

ANAIS NIN: THE MAGIC CIRCLES WEEKEND

And, finally, words from Anais Nin, whose person was the beginning, center, and end-purpose of this book as well as of this Celebration confirming the infinite circular motions of life.

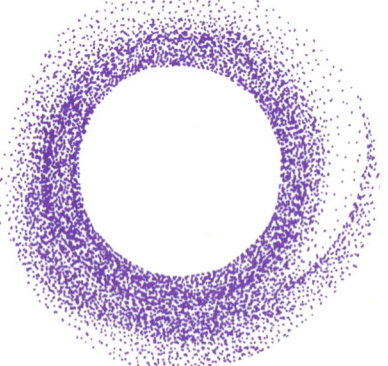

The drive with Beatrice Harris to Rye; Beatrice who has such a deft sense of direction even while we talk of subtle subjects. We want to redefine the much distorted use of narcissism and ego. The isolation which strikes the neurotic at the first shock of destructive experience is not narcissism. It is not a willful isolation and has nothing to do with self-love. It is a withdrawal to rescue what is left of a shattered self. In the same way, self-development and a quest for self awareness and identity are not ego trips.

We talk about our lives, our friends, but it is always to find the meaning of our lives, our friendships. She has that rare mixture of sensuous presence with intelligence and insight which add luminosity and vibrancy to all she does and says.

The house at Rye with its stately beauty reminded me of the house of "The Wanderer," of Alain Fournier, of times when people had a sense of living space.

The garden was peaceful and led down to Long Island Sound. It is a home, I thought, in which we arrive as guests, and Adele and Valerie standing in the entrance hall to receive us, makes it seem like the hospitality of friends. They were offering champagne, and the fairytale clothes of Sas Colby were displayed on mannequins, setting a mood of color and fantasy.

We are distributed to our rooms by Mr. Hewitt who acts as if he were personally interested in our comfort. I can see the Sound from my window. I can feel the presence of the trees.

Adele Aldridge has placed on my bed a gift of her book illustrating the *I Ching*. A beautiful book with bold and vivid designs, each one a different mood, emotionally appealing. Her work reminded me of the medieval expression "Illuminated manuscript", a lost art, but this was an illuminated manuscript, giving the words of the *I Ching* a face.

Eyes of Adele see more than other eyes, she sees dreams as clearly as others see the trees and sound.

As I came downstairs I see the faces which will later become the faces of those I was corresponding with, whose inner face I knew, and it was my turn to seek the faces of the letters as others seek the face of the *Diaries*, to discover the physical presence of my letter writers. Some were friends already: Daisy Aldan with her ever youthful voice and laughter, Evelyn Hinz with her deep dark eyes which convey all the depth and thoughtfulness of her being, Jeffery Mundy with his airy grace and elusive words, Frances Steloff, with her candid blue eyes and white hair glowing like a pearl.

Others whose letters had such vivid accents of distress and solitude: Bebe Herring, tall and beautiful, all eyes too, and Lex Crocker, with his open, warm face and eloquent silences. His letters were moving and deep with feeling.

Bebe Herring gave me the Welsh word, *furrawn*, which means "talk that leads to intimacy." It had inspired all my lectures this year.

Elaine Marks, stood out in my mind as sitting on the front row when Anna Balakian read her essay on my work, nodding her head in approval of Anna's dazzling study.

Trew Bennett, who had written me such spontaneous and confiding letters about her work and her inner journey, now stood before me as beautiful as her letters, whole, with perfect features, so open and tinged with a sadness which never turned to anger or bitterness. The sadness cast her features in a firm, well-balanced beauty. She bears the mark of sorrowing without distortion; it is a mark of courage, of complete sincerity. Her pottery is strong and rich in color.

Jeffery delights in juggling words, in mystifying, in eluding finite meaning. He and his brother seem like two aspects of the same being, both handsome, Jeffery more tenuous, more vaporous, James more grounded, more present, not so prone to take flights in space.

Nadine is silent, but in her silences, conveys thoughtfulness, inner activity, and one is curious to know her world, but I knew it would take time, and the weekend was so full and rich it did not allow me to stay with any one person long enough. I was making a super-human effort of memory, to fuse the person standing before me with the letters received, to reconstruct the exchange that I want to renew and continue. I do not know why I feel that recognizing others, hearing them, sensing them, is so important to life. Too many of us pass in anonymity, invisible, unheard, and I wanted so much to receive all of them. I feel like a gardener concerned with the thirst of flowers, the leaf in danger of withering, the fruit torn off the tree by the wind.

Human beings appear vulnerable, and with great needs. My antennae were spinning furiously to catch all the messages and leave none unheard, but there were so many that I am sure I failed. I read their eyes, I notice when Evelyn sits alone and wonder if she feels isolated, has not found a friend yet. I want to hear every word and receive every message.

Our first evening in the library, when I wanted so much to know them, and they talked about the effect of my work, I felt wistful. The role of the writer forces her to speak for others, and I wanted to hear their voices. I had to accept that my diary was theirs, that they found themselves in it, their voice, and that they were speaking through my work, making revelations about themselves.

I am moved by the response to my work, the statements made as to its significance at crucial moments of their lives. I wanted them to introduce themselves, and what they told me was of their encounter with my work, and its impact, so I have to speak about their revealing themselves to me through my words, and my being their voice.

Happenings begin. The walls are covered with paintings. I notice some large blue sea and sky paintings. I notice masks of iron, abstract and very modern. The face and the cage-like mask interplay, part face, part mask. The sculptor Suzanne Benton is there and later she will talk about the masks while we try them on and see ourselves transformed. The hand printed books are in a glass cabinet, and we will talk about them later.

Valerie effaced herself. She was attentive to the flow and continuity, and to the forming of links. She was protective and receptive, asking nothing for herself, running through her slides too quickly for us to seize the intention of her book, a study of the fears which hamper women artists.

At times the whole weekend appeared like a ballet. Everyone brought charms, skills, richness, and we moved about discovering each other, we discovered each other's struggles, evolutions, achievements. We touched, contacted. But I could not select one and go off for a walk, or select two and talk all night; I had a more difficult task which was to respond to all. With all my passion for knowing others, I sought in the few moments given us to perceive a whole life, a whole person. I talked with Trew Bennett, with Lex Crocker, with Bebe, with William Claire, with Georgiana Peacher who is designing and writing a beautiful book, with Helen Bidwell, with Lele Stephens, and others.

The next morning (I was the only one whose body refused to stay up all night) I was up early, at six a.m. I saw Trew sitting out by the water's edge, writing, and I wanted to go out and talk with her, but I had manuscripts to read, Jeffery's poetry, Bebe Herring's novel, poems.

As I came down the curved stairway Bebe was sitting in a nook, in the sun drenched stairs, with her large questioning eyes. We talked about her novel, her struggle to fuse fiction and non-fiction. She was dressed in a long flower-colored dress, she seemed like part of the garden, a nymph.

During the talk in the library on women's liberation, Beatrice brought her skill at balancing contradictory and extreme generalizations. She restored symmetry and harmony in ideas carelessly incomplete.

It was then that Larry Sheehan spoke movingly and humanly. He said that it was concern for his daughter's future which made him open to the efforts of women to change women's status. He became aware that his daughter might live in a better world. It was a human and humble and touching concept.

Frances Steloff sat gazing at a yellow daisy, her white hair luminous, holding her eyes down, looking into the heart of the flower while telling her story of courage and audacity.

She told the whole story of the birth of the Gotham Book Mart, with a capital of $100. She came away with a new awareness of the importance of the Gotham Book Mart in the literary history of America. Every story we told during the weekend ended with: "We took our work to the Gotham Book Mart and Frances Steloff agreed to sell it."

William Claire told the story of "Voyages," that of a man occupied by a full time job, writing poetry on yellow pads during interminable conferences, and persisting in publishing only what he liked. He had the courage to turn down a bad poem by a famous poet, something very few editors are capable of.

Color and playfulness were given by Sas Colby. We all tried on her capes, skirts, masks, but when we sat in the garden they came to a life of their own when she put them on, with her pixie face and blond hair, acting out a semidance, skits of her own making, brief airy lines, humorous and in harmony with her clothes.

Anna Balakian read a penetrating essay on my work. By way of symbolism and surrealism, she developed the genesis of the work and its ultimate significance. She opened the very heart of the work. Everyone gasped and begged for a copy. I was close to tears at her understanding and evaluation.

The evolutions of friendships, of exchanges, of communication through one's work, were warm and continuous. Everyone was writing; I found manuscripts at my door, poems and letters on my bed. The happenings were necessary to our knowledge of each other's work, but after that was done, we could have lived together for many weekends and not exhausted all we had to say to each other. Most of them (as I had before the diaries were published) had suffered from isolation and loneliness. This was a banquet. I love the French expression "liante", which means connecting as the branches of the ivy do. In French they say she is "liante" or not "liante". "Liante", liana, a beautiful word. It could have been the keyword of the weekend. An atmosphere was created by Valerie and Adele and Larry, of faith and appreciation and encouragement and response. I felt joyful that my work had made the links, and that I could lie back and enjoy the miracle. They were writing, they were walking together, talking together, they were exchanging books, they were living and I could rest as after giving birth. I was being thanked. But I did not want to rest. I wanted to talk at length with everyone, to read all the writing. I couldn't. My body could not. At midnight I was asleep. The life current was strong. It belongs to them now. There was in me a wistful relinquishing dictated by the body, but the receptivity never ceases, as if I were responsible for sustaining the life force. I could sleep. I felt I was inside of my diaries, enclosing new friends, new faces.

There was another beautiful young woman who had come to me at Green Bay in tears. Moira Collins. She is here, clear eyed, graceful.

I was reminded of my envy of the life of George Sand, when distances by carriage were so great from Paris to country homes that friends visited for long periods. They wrote books, put on plays, worked all day but gathered in the evenings, and I thought how wonderful then to have such long deep days with others when modern life makes our meetings brief and fleeting and travel disperses us.

Here we just had time to begin friendships, to give each other courage. They gave me courage. I was moved when Joan Anacreon stood up during one of the dinners and read with great emotion of a poem saying YES YES YES.

I may have been the catalyst, but the radiations of the circle extended far, and each circle gained momentum from the contributions of others. Jeffery shed light and charm, Nadine read her music-filled novel, Beatrice clarified tangled thoughts, and left confirmed of her own desire to write.

I came away convinced I had found a way to sustain life and creation, and this selection of people proved it; it was filled with talent, skills, beauty.

Everything I ever gave was returned to me. We gave birth to each other.

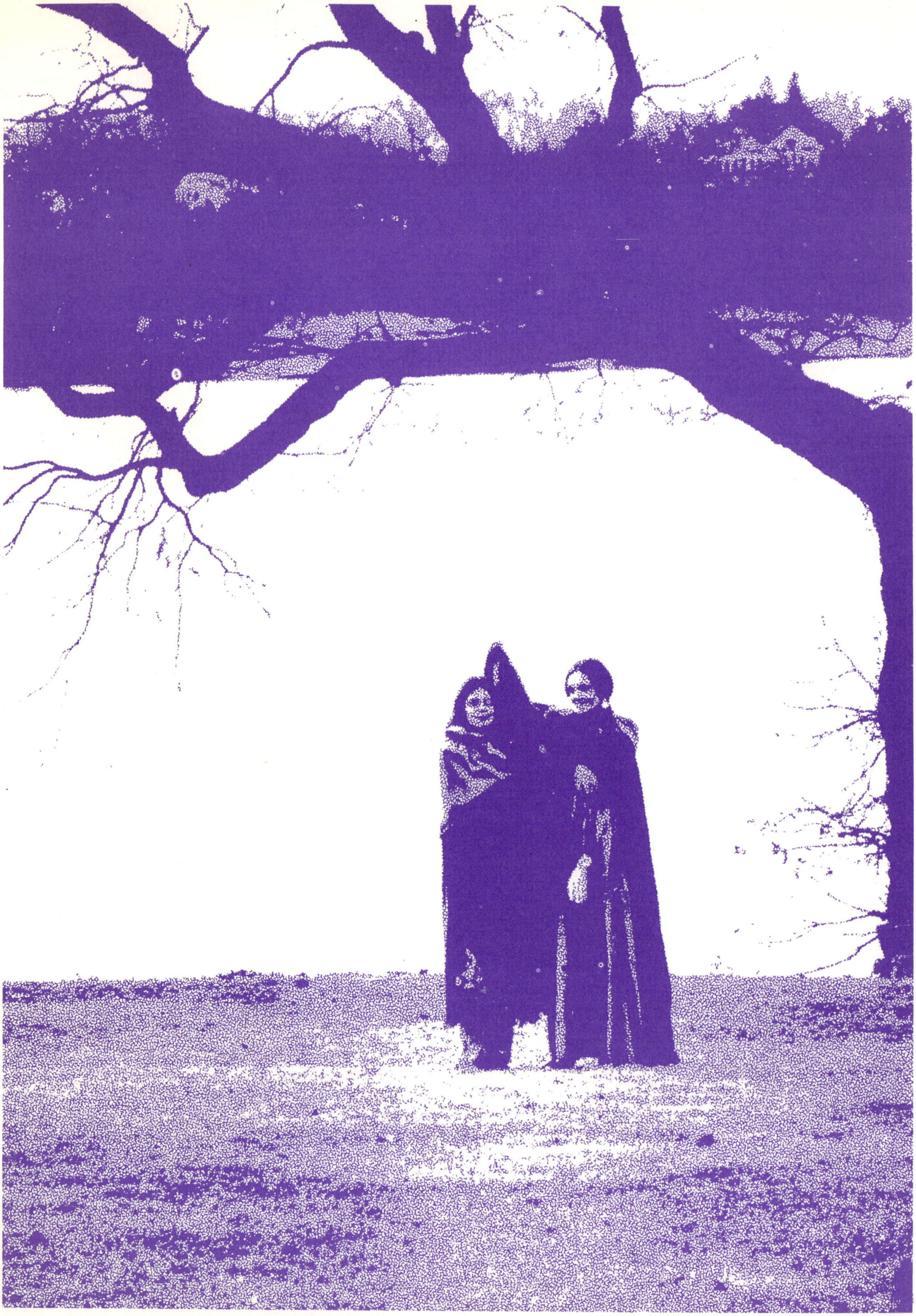